I0006997

Working in IT

Rob England

Sensible business practices

Created by Two Hills Ltd

letterbox@twohills.co.nz

www.twohills.co.nz

PO Box 57-150, Mana
Porirua 5247
New Zealand

© Copyright Two Hills Ltd 2009

Published by Two Hills
First published 2009

ISBN: 1442129999

EAN-13: 978-1442129993

Cover: Pukerua Bay, New Zealand.
Photos by the author.

Although this book has been carefully prepared, neither the author nor the publisher accepts
any liability for damages caused by any error or omission of this book.

Dedicated to IT people everywhere, especially the geeks.

Contents

Introduction

Rob England is best known as the IT Skeptic, an online gadfly to the IT industry. But in a past life he spent a lot of time developing and delivering professional development training for software consultants for one of the world's largest software companies, Computer Associates, now known as CA, and managing a team of those same consultants.

As an entity CA has some interesting attitudes to staff relations and staff training, but the Australian subsidiary had its own culture once, and a free hand to develop staff programs. Rob conceived, designed, developed and delivered training to over 80 staff. Feedback from attendees and their managers was generally positive and the program was judged a success. For some people it was life-changing.

Rob is now an author and commentator, and that experience has come through in a number of articles Rob has published on sites such as IT Career Planet and Datamation, as well as on the IT Skeptic blog www.itskeptic.org, and on his other websites such as www.ttjasi.org and www.ops4less.com and even his personal www.bothol.org. He is working on a new book for 2009, *He Tangata, IT is the People*[1] which will focus on cultural change within IT.

This book is a collection of Rob's writing about IT careers and professionalism (including some unpublished material): collated, edited and improved. Very little of this material has appeared in any of Rob's other books. Admittedly it is a bit of a grab-bag: it reflects the author's own experiences and inspirations, it does not set out to be a comprehensive survey of the topics. Here you will find ideas and inspiration to think about your own career and the careers of those who work for you, and to make a difference in both.

---

[1] see www.itskeptic.org/hetangata

Technical careers

What matters

When one spends 50 or 60 hours a week immersed in an activity (does anyone reading this still work 40 hours or less?), it is easy to lose one's perspective on just where that activity should rate in our lives.

Especially for those of us who work in IT, with its high levels of pressure, responsibility and accountability (at least in the ideal model, even if they are often avoided in practice – see *The Success of Mediocrity*).

For some of us, that very responsibility gives us a sense of importance, belonging and purpose – people depend on us. Our pager or mobile phone proves it by ringing us at all hours and in all places. We take the call because that shows others just how essential we are. It is very like the focus to our lives that children give. It may well be the same emotional pathways that are being invoked.

The danger of course is that, given the duration and intensity of the work experience, we can easily lose sight of the rest of our lives. Maybe other aspects of life lack the buzz and the rewards of time at work, but that will never change if we neglect them.

There is a road called the Karakoram Highway, a wild military road punched through an arm of the Himalayas by the Chinese army at the cost of 900 lives to connect to their ally Pakistan.

It winds up the beautiful Hunza valley full of warring Islamic tribes before trekking across the plateau wastes of Xinshiang to remote Kashi, populated by the more peaceful but equally hard-bitten Uygur people. It is not a road I expected to share with a portly young earth-mother from Hawaii, robed in velvet kaftan and dripping chunky jewellery, with two little blond pre-school children in tow.

Now at the time my pony tail came halfway down my back and nobody could have guessed my natural skin colour, so I liked to think I was travel-hardened and open-minded, but I struggled with the idea of those two kids staying in the same roadhouses and eating in the same markets and scrambling onto the same local buses as me.

I challenged her on it, and I learned something of great value. She said that it was not a decision she liked to take – bringing them there - but it was the right one because it fit her priorities.

So long as you have your priorities clearly sorted, then decisions are easy, even the hard ones. Her number one priority was travel, number two was the children. She went through the angst of making that choice once, then every decision followed naturally. She was going to travel, therefore she made what arrangements she could to ensure the safety and happiness of the kids as they came along. They were as knowledgeable about food-safety, stranger-danger and self-doctoring as I was. They were a tough worldly road-warrior pair. Now you or I may not agree with her choice, but I believe her methodology was sound.

Take the time to decide your priorities, and review them every few years or at any life-changing event. Write them down, ranked from 1 downwards. Give it proper time and effort – do it properly and honestly. No equals. Be realistic, honest and at times brutal. Don't write what you think they should be, write what they really are.

Get at least the top half dozen clear and settled – the rest don't matter so much, though it is good to be clear on what comes at the bottom too. If you get stuck, try getting a couple of trusted friends together for an evening or a day to help each other develop your priority lists.

For example, mine are:

- Security and happiness of my nuclear family: my wife, son, mother, and sister.
- My son's growth, development and education.
- Our home.
- Travel and other novel experiences
- Self-expression, for example through writing or creative hobbies.
- Living a long life. The older I get, the more that deferring death creeps up this list. So far it is working.
- Security and happiness of my extended family.
- Mental health, especially time out in the wild, back to nature.
- Friends.
- Preserving heritage, especially my family's.
- ... [many omitted here]
- Earning money, though it gets higher attention where it facilitates higher priorities.
- ... [many omitted here]
- Watching TV, movies, DVDs, reading papers and magazines, consuming podcasts blogs and websites, music or any of the other media barrages that try to jelly our brains, except as necessary for something above.
- Mowing the lawn.
- Social change. I long since lost my boyish desire to fix the world. I've come to terms with it, I'm open about it.
- Politics. [End of list]

Your job has two aspects that may well appear in different places on the list; what you do because you want to, and what you do because you need the money to pay for what you want. You will note that working appears only briefly as part of number 5 on my top 10 priorities, other than as a means to obtain the money to pay for them. So why did I once allow it to consume more than half my waking hours (even including weekends)?

That noted philosopher, Garfield the cat, said "Work is so bad they have to pay you to do it". Arrange your life so that work gets the priority it deserves based on your list, and so that it leaves sufficient room and resources for your other priorities to get proper attention.

What is important

My wife had breast cancer. It had got into the lymph nodes and come within three millimetres of the chest wall when Burton took a knife to her. He cut her breast off, cut out an evil alien life-form that was growing to consume her in a painful death, and then he sewed her back up without killing her.

Then Peter poisoned her. He pumped her full of toxins so vile the nurses administering them had safety procedures not to get them on anyone's skin. He killed parts of her without killing all of her.

People like Burton and Peter save so many lives we are in danger of losing sight of what it is they do, of passing by and rushing on. I looked at Burton one day when the two of us were alone in his office, and I said "I can't imagine what it is like to be you. While I get paid as much as you to persuade people to spend other people's money to buy software they don't need, you get up every morning and save people's lives by cutting them apart. I can't begin to imagine how it feels to be you". He just smiled a shy smile and changed the subject: the man is a saint.

What is it like? Is it a frightening responsibility? A grind? A burden, an inescapable curse? Just a job? Satisfaction we mortals can only dream of?

They make mistakes. What happens when someone dies? Do they just think "Oops! Better not do it that way again"? I doubt it. Try to imagine how it feels to get up the next morning, hopefully not take it out on the spouse and kids, and go back to work to try again.

Stop now and ponder how it might be to be Burton, and give thanks people like him are about.

The next time a boss is going on about how important this deal or project is, tell them (or yourself, depending on your relationship and career plans) no it isn't. It bloody isn't. What Burton and Peter do is important, especially when it is you they are trying not to kill.

In "What Matters", p9, we talked about listing your personal priorities. Less important than what Burton does but just as important to you personally are all the other things you put on that priority list *above work*. Once you have those priorities clear, the decision on whether to work the weekend becomes much easier.

Employers think they have the right to make you do anything they want. They don't. They buy your consent, and you can withdraw your consent any time you want.

Once upon a time there was a tacit contract of loyalty between employer and employee: serve the company well and have a job for life, and stand by each other if you or the company falls on hard times. In the last thirty years, companies worldwide have demonstrated clearly just how much loyalty they have to their people: none at all. It is all about shareholder value now, and good loyal people are as expendable as office furniture.

For those in a big corporation: the next time your CEO gets paid their annual salary and bonus, do the maths. I worked for a software company that paid $1.1 billion to the top three execs in a single year in bonuses alone (as an aside, some of that was clawed back by shareholders and one of the three is now in jail). Add in their salaries, stock and other benefits, and we are talking in excess of $2 billion.

This was some of the most grotesque pillaging in corporate history, but it is an extreme example of the kind of thing that goes on all the time. Here is the calculation I did at the time: $2B / 15,000 employees = $133,000 for every single employee in the firm. In one year. Next time your CEO goes on about how "you guys are our company's most valuable asset", say (again: to yourself or out loud) "how about just half of that fat cheque for us then?"

If you do the exercise of the list of priorities, but do it for your organization instead of yourself, in 95% of organizations you will see that employees are not the most important asset at all. In that company I worked in, the maintenance stream of the existing customers is the most important asset, followed by the copyright and patents on the software code. Next would come brand then probably facilities.

If employees are expendable, so are employers. The new generation of workers is not afraid to walk: if you are under 30 I'm preaching to the converted here. For the rest of you, get wise. Be prepared to tell them "take this job and shove it", in the words of the old song. In fact TTJASI has become an acronym in common use, and evolved into a slang word "ttjasi". Don't be afraid to do a ttjasi[1].

Another good line is "work to live, don't live to work". Some people do a job they hate, to pay for a life they like. That's cool, if that supports your priorities. What is uncool is when work prevents you from meeting your higher priorities. That is when you get work out of the way: when work has become more important in your life than it should.

---

[1] Ttjasi, v. the act of quitting your job. An acronym for *Take This Job And Shove It*, a song by David Allan Coe, made famous by Johnny Paycheck. See www.ttjasi.org

Where do you rank on the dung-heap?

Any time I get feeling down about not being able to help my in-laws in their developing-nation struggle, or afford the new deck on the house, or take Jack on a trip to ride steam trains in South America or drive the new Millau Viaduct in France, I contemplate where I come on the dung-heap that is the human race.

On the back of an envelope: There are about 400 million in North America and Europe each. Say 300 x2 = 600M of them are middle class or better. Chuck in another three hundred million from China and India combined, and an assorted three hundred million from the rest, and you get about one-and-a-quarter billion living comfortably, out of about eight billion.

So if you are reading this on a home PC in a developed-nation-middle-class standard home, or better, you are already in the top 15% of the human race for prosperity.

Follow this line of reasoning for your own situation, and the majority of my readers will end up feeling pretty good.

You may be quite poor by local standards but you think the country you live in is one of the best, so look at your country's population as a proportion of the world total (this doesn't work so well in India or China). Me I live in New Zealand, and just about everyone in the world wants to live in New Zealand. We have 3M people so already I'm in the top 0.03% !!!

Then you can add time as a dimension to the calculations. Even though each generation is better off, and the bulk of human history has involved lives that were "nasty, brutish and short", one assertion by experts is that over half the people who have ever lived on the planet are alive right now. [Thus arguing that reincarnation is the product of fevered imaginations]. So adding in all those who have gone before doesn't change the numbers as much as you might think. Allowing for a few people who were nicely off in the past, call it a total of 14 billion instead of 8 in your divisor.

At the other extreme a number that gets bandied about is 40 billion total. Use that as a divisor to make yourself feel real good.

The commoditisation of the technical profession

Generations ago, the career ambitions of an intelligent and ambitious geeky young man (we're talking pre-women's–lib) might well have included such demanding and technically advanced professions as steam engine driver or typist or telephone operator. The technically inclined among their children and grandchildren aspired to be business machine mechanics, electricians, and then computer operators. A generation ago, leading edge roles for young persons included programmer, or – for the elite – systems programmer or database administrator. Then it was network administrator or communications architect or web designer.

The relentless advance of the technological revolution over centuries creates an interesting phenomenon in the technical professions that doesn't happen (at least as markedly) to other professional areas such as law or finance or even medicine: jobs become commoditised.

In part this is because they become semi-automated, or at least the interfaces become easier to learn and use. Database administration is not the arcane art it was with say IMS[1] or IDMS[2] [you kids go look them up]. Even Oracle is easier to run... slightly.

At least as important is that the technical sophistication of each generation of workers stands on the shoulders of those who came before. A typewriter isn't any easier to use today than when first invented. Word processing is much more complex and intellectually demanding than hammering away at mechanical keys. Yet my son was using MS-Word at age 6.

---

[1] http://en.wikipedia.org/wiki/Information_Management_System
[2] http://en.wikipedia.org/wiki/IDMS

The third factor at work is that elite specialist technical professions hide their IP behind a shroud of mystery and jargon. They maintain a Masonic priesthood. Only the invited get the training. Over time this gets stripped away as the knowledge is taught in mainstream education. Think MCSE.

Fourth and last is that some jobs just fall from prominence as they get displaced by new technology: think CICS programmer. Yes I know the few that remain command high prices but this is a market aberration because too many dismissed it too early and the IBM mainframe stubbornly refuses to die (might be something to do with the way it continues to offer efficient, effective, robust processing of transactions year on year). CICS programming is probably not a smart career choice, and eventually the occupation's value will fall to zero.

At the risk of banging on at a theme I've discussed before, there is a great exposure here for technical people. One day you are the highly-paid hero. Then your kids go to school, you build a new house, you change companies a couple of times... and you turn around one day and the salaries are falling as every kid out of college can do your job.

This is a particular danger for those who launch out as consultants based on an extremely marketable skill. That is fine if you are five years from retirement. It is not so fine if you are young.

The smart ones reinvent themselves. They watch the trends, sniff the winds of change. They take the opportunities that come along to learn new skills in the right directions. They jump from the downhill side of one occupation's lifecycle to the upward rise of another's.

So keep a weather-eye on your chosen occupation. Have a plan for your career. Make sure that plan doesn't assume the value of your current skills will continue to increase, or even hold the same level. Advanced technical jobs eventually become commoditised.

How secure is your IT technical career?

If you are a senior (read: over 30) IT technical person, well versed, even expert, in your chosen products and technologies, how secure is your career?

As you get older, you get slower, uglier and more expensive. As your work rate goes down and your cost goes up, you must compensate by expanding your skills and adding more value to the organisation.

Growing more experienced at the same thing isn't enough. After a certain level of experience with technology, more doesn't count for much: enough is enough.

Experience counts for less in the 21st century. The new technologies are not as arcane and inaccessible – it is not a closed priesthood now. In the past, our industry has leant heavily on experience and lightly on qualifications. Once, if someone had a few years on their CV, they could always get a job and ask a lot for it. Now the industry is getting more professional, and certifications and academic backgrounds are beginning to count for more.

It isn't enough to know one technology well any more, or at least it won't be for much longer. Look behind you. There are kids coming up with MCSE[1] or B Sc in object programming or whatever, versed in LDAP[2], Java and Oracle. And those kids are cheaper, keener and smarter than you. Ask yourself frankly: How long would it take a technical school graduate - with the right skills and a few years experience in the industry - to learn enough about your technologies to be able to do a credible job?

---

[1] Microsoft Certified Service Engineer
[2] Never mind

They would get paid a lot less than you to do it, I'll bet. Product technologists are falling down the pecking order (just like programmers and telephonists and typists and steam engineers and every other technology specialist in history). As technologies become commodities, so too do those who work with them.

People who had been with the products for a decade staffed a product support centre I knew in the USA. They were highly experienced, knew every nuance of the software, and had had pay rises every year for that decade. Then the company brought in the "farm boys" (and girls): graduates of rural colleges who couldn't believe their luck in getting a job with a big software company, even if it was at low pay "to begin with". They were smart, and eager to prove their worth. They soon figured out the software well enough to support it. They didn't do as good a job as the old guard, but they were a third the price and they were good enough. And within a few years they were just as good, and all the old guard were gone. This is not a fable.

What is more, the industry is changing. We don't choose technology any more – we create solutions. We aren't tinkering with products: we are engineering systems.

In the past we bought the product and figured out how to make it fulfil the requirement. Now users want to lay out the business requirement and hear how we are going to deliver against it. Features functions and benefits are secondary. They will cover that off at some point. The important question is the deliverable. That deliverable isn't measured in bandwidth or transactions or use cases. It is measured in ROI and timelines and EVA[1], in personal CSF[2]s and industry directions.

If you didn't get my message already, here it is spelt out: if you depend on product and technology expertise alone, you will

---

[1] Economic Value Added
[2] Critical Success Factors

compare less and less favourably against eager cheap young pups wanting a crack at your job on their way up.

A cameraman and his assistant were filming lions on the veldt. The alpha male lion got annoyed and started taking a noticeable interest in them. The cameraman filmed on, then noticed that his assistant had pulled off his heavy boots and was lacing on sneakers. "No point" said the cameraman, "if he decides to go for us you will never out run him". "I don't need to outrun him" replied the assistant, "I only need to outrun you".

The moral of the story is don't film lions. No wait... the moral of the story is to keep an eye on those around you. It may sound brutal but when the 5% layoff tranche comes through, your colleagues are your competitors. Just make sure you are doing more to add value back to the business (and to be seen to add value back to the business) than most of them are. Or at least make sure you are not running at the back of the pack. If you are the highest paid with the narrowest set of skills (don't measure range of technical knowledge – that counts as one skill), then you are walking.

That point about being seen to contribute is important. Technical people are often modest, and take a dim view of those who blow their own trumpet. But ask yourself what the odds are of your manager doing the investigation necessary to get a good picture of who really wrote the document, or who was here over the weekend. Tell them.

And (to jumble analogies) make sure you have a parachute. Where will you work next? Doing what? Make sure your CV looks attractive and your skills are adequate now, before the crunch comes. Being laid off is a traumatic experience: you will cope many times better if you already have a plan and are at least part of the way along the path to being prepared. Better to spend redundancy money on a brief job search and a nice holiday, rather than crammed training and endless door knocking.

Securing your IT career

In a previous article we looked at the position IT technical people find themselves in as technology skills become more of a commodity, and the organisation expects broader skills and greater value back from their higher value IT employees. If you are an IT technical person of increasing seniority (and cost), this article examines your options for staying ahead of the layoffs.

As you get older, you get slower, uglier and more expensive. As your work rate goes down and your cost goes up, you must compensate by expanding your skills and adding more value to the organisation. If you depend on product and technology expertise alone, you will compare less and less favourably against eager cheap young pups wanting a crack at your job on their way up. When the 5% layoff tranche comes through, your colleagues are your competitors. Make sure you are doing more to add value back to the business (and to be seen to add value back to the business) than most of them are.

So where to from here?

More of the same. You can stay a technologist. Get deeper and wider. Stay ahead of the kids. In fact, guide, train and mentor them so you are adding value back. Just accept you won't be the centre of the universe any more.

Management. That is a fine and challenging option if you are good at it. Typically technical people aren't. But by all means have a go: while finding out whether you are suited or not, it will be an enlightening experience. If you really try to embrace the thinking, it will give entirely new perspectives.

Sales. See "Management" above.

Software Engineer. You can grow your engineering skills. Engineers understand how the world works: how systems behave, how problems get solved. They put things together, select components and materials to meet a spec, figure out new ways to use things and to do things. They develop gut instincts for what works, how things scale, how much is needed.

Software Architect. Architecting isn't about selecting which products, or how many servers to put them on. Architecting is about understanding the business requirement in the client's terms, translating that into terms we understand, then working with engineers to determining the best technologies and designs to use to meet that requirement, and to understand how to deliver that.

Business Analyst. A business analyst captures the processes that a company has now and those they want to have, and works out what needs to be done to get from here to there, often but not necessarily in an IT context. If your background is in applications development or process tools, this could be an area of interest for you.

Project Management. Technical people are sometimes systematic and meticulous people, fond of process and detail and doing things properly. If that is you, there will always be a demand for good project managers to ensure successful outcomes. You need the people skills to get things to happen though, and an ability to work in imperfect conditions.

How to get there?

You need to develop yourself. You can do this by growing your thinking through experience, by taking on new roles. You can do it by reading widely, especially periodicals and websites. The Economist and McKinsey Quarterly worked for me. You can do jobs or training that develops different modes of thought, such as sales or management. You can re-educate yourself through something like an MBA, or other tertiary courses.

Don't be daunted by new areas of knowledge. I recall how inaccessible the whole midrange world looked when all I knew was mainframe. Treat any new knowledge domain as just another "product": terms, jargon, rules, models, structures, methods...

What to leave behind

There are aspects of technologists' behaviour which will be intolerable in other roles. Some of these are:

Relish the negative. Technologists love to solve problems and this is a Good Thing. But sometimes that means we love problems for their own sake. And sometimes that means we blow them up or even create them just so we can have the gratification of overcoming them. A smooth path is no fun. But in business, getting to the outcome is everything, preferably with minimum fuss and cost. Something is a problem when it needs to be. It should always be kept in proportion to what really matters.

Be prepared. Technologists like seeking complete information on a problem, being fully knowledgeable in a domain, knowing everything, waiting until prepared. Business isn't Boy Scouts. Real problem solving is about operating with incomplete information, starting before we are ready, failing sometimes, taking risks. If you are building air traffic control or ambulance despatch, it matters. For the rest of us, lighten up and have the courage to fall on your face occasionally.

Tinkering. The hardest part of most other roles is that you seldom get your hands dirty in the technology or get a chance to futz on the Web. Many people manage to keep their hand in ("you can take the boy out of the jungle but you can't take the jungle out of the boy"), but if you are really stretching and growing yourself, you won't have much opportunity.

What can your company do for you?

Obviously any employer needs to be supportive of career development. Make a plan and spell it out to your manager. Seek training that develops different ways of thinking. Look for a mentor: someone you respect who can offer advice and guidance. Learn about how to do mentoring properly. Ask your employer for support and training on a mentoring program. Find out what support is provided for tertiary education.

Start now

How ever you approach your career development, if you are a product technologist you need to break the mould and grow into new areas. If you get complacent and comfortable doing product implementation or support, your status and worth will slowly erode over time. Like the slowly boiled frog, you may not realise the situation you are in until it is too late. Start now: think about where you might like to grow and start heading there.

Who Pays For On-the-Job Training?

Training has always been one of the major staff overheads of the IT industry. In the last decade we have seen the emergence of formal certifications such as CISSP (Certified Information Systems Security Professional), MCSE (Microsoft Certified Systems Engineer), or ITIL Manager (now Diploma). These are highly portable and make valuable additions to one's CV.

Some employers have always provided a lot more training than others, but I think they all will become more reluctant to fund it in coming years. Here's why:

If the loyalty "contract" between employer and employee is not quite extinct, then it is seriously endangered. Decades of shareholder value, human resources, re-engineering, and other changes in the culture of business have seen to that. The number of firms that provide jobs for life, and the number of people who really intend to stay, is dwindling to zero.

IT people always did change jobs more than most industries, but the new Generations X and Y are even more job-mobile than IT people traditionally have been. Employers will see an increasing churn of employees, which means less return on their training investment before that investment walks.

The cost of that investment is increasing. We still have all the proprietary training courses for products and methodologies, but we have also seen the rise of professional certifications which are a good thing for IT professionalism, but don't come cheap.

On the other hand, ongoing training is of increasing importance as rate of change increases. It is no longer enough to get a tertiary qualification, then coast on it until retirement. Continual professional development is essential to stay relevant and employable, in IT more than anywhere.

So who pays?

Employees will find it harder to get a boss to pay. This is not because the boss is a #@$*&%... well it might be, but it also might be simple game strategy. Why should they pay for your training when they can wait for churn to bring them already-qualified job applicants?

As more and more firms twig that they are funding the industry with their training programs, and as more of their competitors start winding back to exploit them, they will be asking staff to have a stake in the game. Investment in training still makes sense, but it will come with provisos. They will ask staff to agree to an indenture for some period, or to pay part of the costs. Expect more employers paying only if you pass!

Therefore it is time you thought about your own training program. It is essential for any professional career and a good idea for anyone who does not intend to be doing the same job until they die. Create a short list of qualifications and certifications that are important for your career. Job advertisements are a good place to start. Consider which training you can get your employers to pay for, or at least contribute to. Start asking for this at review time, while you still can.

For the remainder that they are unlikely to cover, try to put a dollar value on the return you will get from the training. Find out how much more that people earn once they have the certification. For example, see *What's the Most Profitable IT Certification?*[1], and talk to recruiters. Consider too the intangible value: whether it takes you in the direction you plan to go; whether it would get you the projects or promotions you want.

---

[1] http://itmanagement.earthweb.com/career/article.php/3682101

Treat each one as a business proposal – consider the business case and especially the return on investment. Ensure you really will make more money or derive some other value, and that this value exceeds the cost of the training.

For example, I still don't have my ITIL Manager's certification, but it has never stopped me from getting more than enough ITIL consulting work. The day the lack of it starts losing me income is the day I'll start thinking about getting it. Even then, I'll also consider whether there is some cheaper certification or some other use of the funds that would fill the income gap.

That is not to say the ITIL Diploma is a waste of money. It is an excellent investment for some people, such as those who want to break into the profession, or whose employers need a credibility boost in that space [in which case get the boss to pay!].

Build a plan

Build a personal training plan. List what you are going after, how you will fund it, and when you can fit it in. That last item is your final challenge in all this. Most employers will give you time off to go on training, especially if you are paying. Many will even continue to pay you. But not all will let you go in work time, not if you are essential and it becomes their problem to cover you. So you may have to plan to do the training after hours.

If the training is for an extended period, then you have to plan for one of two things: Either arrange to put much of your personal life on hold while you both work and study; or fund a break from working while you study full-time. A good friend did an MBA while working full-time for a big IT vendor while he and his wife had their second child. Beats me how he and the marriage survived. This is not something to enter into lightly.

Once you have a plan, start saving. It helps now; it will soon be essential as employers wake up to just how much of their training investment is walking out the door.

The 7 Top Reasons Why You Can't Quit Your Job

7 You are afraid of the unknown

You are worried about not knowing what will happen to you. You can drive half-a-ton of steel at sixty miles an hour inches away from other vehicles, and trust their drivers to do the same. You can purchase and eat food that you didn't see being cooked. You can enter a convenience store after nightfall.

You regularly plug and unplug cables carrying 120 volts (or 240 volts) of lethal electricity. Heck, you pipe the stuff through a pad in your bed. But changing jobs makes you nervous.

6 It is comfortable where you are.

It may not be great but it is not so bad. Your boss cares about your personal future and is doing everything he/she and the company can do to advance you and set you up for a good retirement.

Your co-workers are all the kind of people you would socialise with anyway even if you didn't work with them. What you do is what you would do as a volunteer. It is more fun at this job than anything else you could be doing.

5 You can't afford a pay-cut or time out of work

If your income were halved this year it would be a disaster. You would fall to nearly the income levels of your parents when they were your age. Only half the third world would want to be you instead of all of them.

No way that half your spending goes on things you could do without for a short while. And the tax benefits would barely cover your annual bar tabs.

4 There is too much competition for work

You're right. An employer is never going to look at you when there are all those people who have been out of a job for years, turned down by dozens of employers already. Employers don't want someone like you who resigned with a plan to better yourself and thinks their job is something you'd be happier at and do a better job of, when they could get cheap workers who are way more desperate.

3 Your partner would kill you

You would be selfish to introduce such uncertainty into your partner's life. Instead of worrying about your personal development, you should be delivering the weekly paycheck. They don't care if you are irritable and restless – better that than getting you all fired up with some scheme to make more money and be happier in the future. A partner who keeps you stable and sensible is more than you deserve.

2 Your parents would kill you

Listen to them. They know that the key to happiness is to land a good job and hang on to it for life. Be loyal to the firm and the firm will be loyal to you. It worked for them and it still works in the 21st Century.

1 You have no right to aspire

You have a job. The majority of the human race don't. Who do you think you are, wanting more? You were put onto this Earth to work and work you shall. You are not here to pursue wisdom or happiness. You are here to produce, to contribute to the social machine. Get over it and get back to your job.

Feeling riled? I hope so. Rip each of these arguments apart then get on and do something about it: ttjasi. You owe it to your future.

How I Downshifted

Once I worked 50-60 hour weeks for an IT vendor. I spent weekend time travelling; I spent 50 or even 100 nights per year away from home; and missed a fair chunk of my son's first four years. My aspirations changed as I got older and had family and the company changed too. It had ceased to be fun. At times it got downright Dilbertesque.

So I quit. Now I work for my own company (I figured it was the only way I was ever going to be a Managing Director). I still work long hours but I do so mostly at home, at times that suit me. I work on projects only if I think they are a good idea. I am away from home when I want. I took most of January off to go camping with my son, and most of February to play with my hobby (model railroading if you must know).

Changing to a lower paced, lower pressure, simpler lifestyle is known as "downshifting". For many people in developed nations, especially those of us in IT, we have sufficient surplus affluence to make it a viable option.

If that sounds like something you would like to do, there are two ways to achieve it. Either (a) make such a bucket-load of money that you need never work again or (b) follow these steps:

1) Freehold your home

Plenty of people go out on their own while still paying mortgage or rent, but if you want to relax a little, downshift, and not be a slave to the job, then you need the freedom of a freehold home. You could go live in a cardboard box, or you could make enough money to pay the mortgage off (see (a) above). It is amazing how quickly some people can clear a mortgage if they set their mind to it, especially childless couples. Alternatively, consider downshifting where you live. If you want the bright lights of the big city, it will be hard for you to escape debt. But if you go live somewhere less hectic you can also find lower property prices: moving from a major city to a smaller town or city can give you enough equity to buy for cash – we did. This does of course require you to...

2) Reduce expectations

People addicted to the high-spend lifestyle that many jobs can buy will remain job-slaves. It is a great help if you can shift to a less materialistic mindset where you value quality family time, peaceful environment, and simple pleasures over dining, travel, fine possessions and inner-city excitement. We can go camping for weeks for the price of one airfare to Bali. Besides, we already have lots of those possessions.

3) Build the right skills

Most IT people after a decade in the industry have plenty of bankable technical skills. The key skills that many lack are an understanding of business and of consulting. These can be learnt. Pursuing this line of personal growth will serve you well whether you stay with your employer (see Strategies for Securing Your IT Career) or go out on your own, so your employer should be supportive of this direction and it does not commit you to a decision.

4) Realise your value

For most IT people, what you can make per hour as an independent consultant is several times what your boss is paying you per hour. So even with down-time and no paid holidays, you can work for less hours and still be in the same financial shape – or good enough shape (see Reduce Expectations, above).

If you don't want to work by the hour at all, you can try your hand as an entrepreneur. That would require you to...

5) Consider taking a risk

The only difference between successful entrepreneurs and other folk is a comfort with risk. They may not thrive on it, or even like it, but they all can live with it. You can make a lot of money working for a salary or for contracts but the only way to get stinking rich is to derive income from something that scales, i.e. something that is not linked to the number of hours you have in a day. This could be selling a product or an idea, trading, or getting other people to work for you. These are all entrepreneurial activities, and they involve higher potential rewards and higher risks.

Paid by the hour you have a good idea how much you will be making in ten years time. One catalyst for my downshift was a report from a financial planner who said I only had another eleven years to go before I would have enough saved to downshift to a lower-income job and still have a secure retirement. Eleven years at that job was not an attractive option. About the same time my father dropped dead. So did a neighbour younger than I. That was it! If I was to get any lifestyle other than grinding away for a third decade as a salary-slave, I had to take a gamble.

The gamble is to become an entrepreneur. Never mind the details (get your own ideas). By chasing business ideas and opportunities my future income is less determinate but potentially much higher.

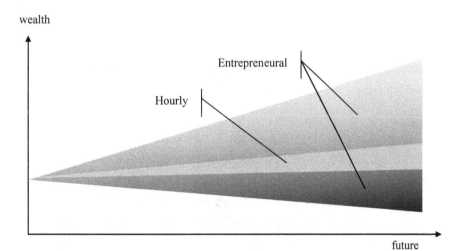

I can make enough money from occasional odd-jobbing contracts to keep us alive and still have many months a year to spare to work on various projects. So I give myself five years to make two million dollars. If I succeed I retire; if I fail, I start my eleven year grind five years late. Not attractive but hardly the end of the world.

To do this you must be ready to fail, or to make a loss. This may not sound like downshifting, and for many it isn't. If not, stop at step 4. For some of us, the ability to accommodate calculated risk gives us the flexibility, freedom and creative excitement that our previous lives lacked.

Downshifting is a leap of faith. It takes courage, preparation and a belief in yourself. The rewards are worth it... I think. Ask me in four years.

Four years later I say yes they are still worth it. Even with the 2009 recession, even though we are as poor as we ever want to be, I'm still not as stressed as I was on the corporate treadmill. And I'm definitely not as miserable. In fact I'm having an unreasonably good time, considering how parlous our position is. That two million is no closer but I'm having fun trying.

Downside to downshift

Nothing is perfect. Any improvement comes at a cost. What can downshifting cost you?

Money

As we said, you need to have lower expectations of income and wealth. You just might end up better off, but don't plan on it. The corollary to reduced income is ironically reduced freedom in one respect; I miss the freedom to go anywhere in the world I want, and I miss the freedom to buy anything I see. I give up these freedoms in return for freedom of time and freedom from authority and freedom from b.s. emails from management and Marketing.

Security

Consulting can be a nerve-wracking game when things are slow and you cannot see where the next job is coming from. Running a business is even more so. You need to have the confidence that you will always be able to turn a buck, even if it is a much-reduced income that just meets your much-reduced expectations.

Development

Without a big organisational nanny, you must see to your own training and growth.

Golden handcuffs

By not giving me continuance of service when I changed countries my employer made the decision easy for me by taking away any golden handcuffs. For others it is hard to walk away from potential redundancy payments. If you really want to be free, you have to see it as unreal money, and go after the real money you can make for yourself.

World's toughest boss

Sometimes I wish I worked for anyone other than myself.

"Internet I gave you all the best years of my life..."

The world is full of those chasing fame and fortune on the internet. The glittering lures of e-commerce, Adsense and cult-herodom draw them from far and wide, looking for easy money, good hours and groupies. It is not like that.

Just like the rock-and-roll industry has its Rolling Stones, Madonna and Led Zeppelin, the internet examples are all there for us. Tim Ferriss achieves widespread fame with his (excellent) book and website *The Four-Hour Work Week*. Manolo's Shoe Blog is reputed to pull six figures a year. And of course Mark Zuckerberg at the ripe old age of 22 turns down a **billion** dollars for Facebook.

Just like the music industry, the reality may not match the legends. Many of these reports come from those who profit from the frenzy in the industry – objectivity is often questionable. And just like music, for every shooting star there are thousands of wanna-bes banging away in seedy bars while holding down a day job.

Internet entrepreneurship is very like pop music. If Sony knew for sure how to engineer a hit they would only publish a few CDs a year. The model is that you keep throwing them at the wall and see what sticks. Same with websites. So many aspiring webpreneurs seek that one great idea that will go platinum, like Craigslist or Skype or Facebook or Digg or YouTube or Wikipedia or MegaUpload or GameFAQs or so many others.

I have my favourite examples, where I think "dang, I should have thought of that!" These include Neopets, tinyURL, Wikia, MissBimbo and The New York Times.

(Just kidding about that last one, but let us consider it for a moment. It illustrates the point that along with the internet poster-children of pure e-commerce, there is another large group of sites that succeeds on the internet because they are just another channel to a successful bricks-and-mortar business.

(Contrary to common assumption, Amazon is more part of this latter group. Even though it was born from the internet it needs serious real-world infrastructure investment and management, so I do not consider it a pure internet play. Other examples are CafePress and Lulu.)

But for every success there are thousands of failures. Right now my most successful site has a traffic rank on Alexa of 1,341,140. That's right – it is on its way to being the millionth-most-popular site on the Web.

Blogging is the latest big thing: we'll all grow rich by exposing our brilliance and wit to the world, who will come in droves to click on Adsense links and product referrals. ProBlogger tells us about the six-figure sites, but Technorati tells me they are "currently tracking 112.8 million blogs". The odds are against us.

The ones who really get rich in the music industry are the venue owners, publishers and promoters. In the same way the big winners on the internet are the advertising middlemen like Google, and the myriad hosting companies. Thousands of aspirants risk their time and money each month chasing success and almost all of them lose.

I have a site that has a Google page rank of five, and it draws tens of thousands of page views a month. It pays me over a hundred dollars a month, heading towards two hundred. If I charged the time I spent on it at my usual IT consulting rate it would owe me over a hundred thousand dollars. That isn't good ROI.

Many hopeful rock bands spend tens of thousands on instruments and amps and lighting, then can't get a gig. Recently on www.websitebroker.com a site was offered for sale: "...This website cost a little over $20,000 to develop. It is a complete Flash 8 video streaming website with a content management system and registration system ... Price: $8,000". This is even worse ROI – real money gone.

And then there are the dreamers. Successful entrepreneurship requires good business sense and gritty pragmatism. How about this ad on www.buysellwebsite.com "...currently developing a video game trading site which will allow users to trade video games with each other...Are there sites like this already? Yes, I have seen a couple and they all make money and you can too if you market it properly... Price: $60,000" – for an unfinished site entering a market with established competitors.

Most sites for sale go for a few hundred or at most a few thousand dollars, so don't go spending tens of thousands on developers and designers. Launch the site as rough and ugly as you can and just test the waters to see if anyone actually cares – the equivalent of banging out a few numbers at the local pub on a Saturday night to see whether the crowd produces cheers or bottles. AdWords is a superb medium for testing ideas and marketing for a very low cost – you only pay if they click so lousy ideas cost you nothing!

If the crowd loves it and you take off, then you can use the revenue to pay for the fancy stuff in a self-fuelling process that will grow readership. Dump the sleazy manager you started with and find some classy gigs to play at. That is, move on from Adsense and DirtCheapHosting.com to targeted advertising services and robust hosting platforms.

Until then don't give up your day job.

Professionalism

A third of the population is incompetent

Talking to the electrician one day about how hard it is to get good service, he said "I'm convinced a third of the public is incompetent".

Actually I was talking to the back of his head and the infamous tradesman's bum-crack[1] as he crouched over a wall outlet rewiring it before it burned our house down. When he made the statement about "...a third ...is incompetent" I agreed and we had a good bitch about how hopeless clerical and trades and service people are.

But later as I pondered the point that "...a third ...is incompetent" it occurred to me that I had bought into the same statistical fallacy that I lambasted McKinsey for in a blog post over on the IT Skeptic blog some time ago.

I said:

> what is it about analysts' inability to understand basic statistics?
>
> "only 34 percent say that they are more effective at introducing new technologies than their competitors are" is like saying "only 34% are tall". Well, duh! It's a bit sad when supposed business gurus can't grasp the concept of a bell curve.

...which makes it even sadder when I fall down the same hole.

Competence (or conversely, incompetence) is a relative term. Everyone makes mistakes, no-one is infallible (notwithstanding

---

[1] Cultural note: I don't know about your country but in New Zealand (and Australia) most tradesmen wear shorts. Most tradesmen think they are still a size L. So most tradesmen tend to spill over the top of their shorts when bending over. It is a major source of visual pollution in my country, and a famous phenomenon much commented upon.

papal claims), so no-one is perfectly competent, although some seem to be perfectly incompetent. One is competent as measured against the norm or average of the population. So assuming an approximately normal (i.e. bell curve) distribution, about a third is more competent than average, about a third is around average, and about a third is indeed incompetent.

And about a third always will be, no matter how we educate, thrash or genetically engineer the population.

England's Corollary to this conclusion: when they look for people to do the tedious, thankless, stressful jobs of facing the customer, and they pay little for it, anyone who can get a job somewhere else does so. Guess which third their recruits most likely come from?

A depressing thought: I will continue to suffer cock-ups by my bank, insurance companies, tradespeople, and of course government for ever because a third of the population is incompetent and service jobs suck so badly only the incompetent third take them.

And how many trickle into the IT profession because...

We give anyone a go in IT

In the current job market [*pre-2009*], the IT industry will take anyone it can get. No wonder we have such a woeful track record for delivering or managing systems.

Imagine this scenario: Joe drives a concrete mixer. He gets a job with a construction company who make bridges. Mostly they make small overpasses where most of the concrete goes into the abutments and retaining walls, and the actual spans are steel girders. Once or twice he is there when they pour a concrete span. Joe sometimes talks to the onsite engineers. The engineers onsite are juniors. They have a university degree in structural and/or civil engineering. They are serving their time to get enough experience to get back in the office where the real work of designing the bridges goes on. From the engineers Joe picks up the terminology and some rudiments of the theory of bridge design. He learns about the steel reinforcing, about what can and can't be done with concrete. At one point Joe even takes three days off work to do an adult education class on "Foundations of Bridge Design and Construction" for which they gave him a multi-choice test and a nice certificate at the end.

After fifteen years driving trucks they make Joe the leading hand. He still delivers but he gets to boss four other drivers around. Despite the promotion, Joe decides he has had enough of driving trucks. Engineering is the way to go. He scans the job ads.

Meanwhile across town the government wants to build a new four-lane road bridge across the river. They engage a small consulting firm who are not well known but have the advantage of being cheap and local. The firm is already up to its ears in projects so they advertise for an engineer to manage the project and develop the design. There is a great shortage of engineers and the only application is from Joe. His CV reads, in part:

After fifteen years in the bridge construction industry in a variety of roles, Joe feels ready to take on a more senior position ...

Experience:

Joe worked on more than seventy major bridge construction projects including the following three concrete span constructions...

Positions:

Concrete materials facilitator 1992-2007

Manager concrete deployment division 2007-2008

Qualifications:

Certificate in Structural Engineering

After two interviews (for which Joe bought a suit), they hire Joe without reference checks and without investigating the institute issuing the "certificate" or the nature and extent of the study. He knows what he is talking about; he has worked with every type of concrete there is; he's been there on projects they respect; and he knows quite a few people in the industry.

When Joe arrives on the job, he has never heard of the standard book of tables and bridge designs, so he gets out pencil and paper and starts making a few sketches...

This would never happen. But the equivalent happens regularly in the IT industry. How familiar do these stories sound?

Bill started life as an operator on MVS mainframes. After ten years in his first job, he was moved to a systems programming role where the company trained him in CICS and COBOL. Since then he has moved jobs every 18 months to three years. His growing list of projects and systems means his CV gets him a job just about anywhere, but funnily enough he never stays long...

Ann worked her way up the Finance division of a large organisation to become CFO. When the IT department hit new lows of budget blowouts and failures to deliver, she replaced the rapidly exiting CIO. She never had much interest in technology but she knows how to develop her own spreadsheets and has created a number of Access databases for asset management and financial reporting.

Michael graduated in computer science from a college in a small Caribbean nation, where he learned VB and Pascal, writing programs for address books and online games. A US company gave him an internship on pittance pay, promising a green card. After three years the green card finally happened. Not long afterwards he left, using his experience writing VB to get a lead role on a software design team creating a new safety control system.

Susan qualified as an accountant, worked regularly with an accounting software package, got a job with a consulting firm selling and supporting it in her area, then parlayed this experience in IT to get a job on a multi-million dollar project implementing the package in a corporation.

Ralph got a job here twenty-five years ago when there was one computer and we programmed it with cards. Nobody knows what he did before. He's been here ever since. Now he manages the UNIX servers. They fall down a lot and software upgrades have fallen several years behind, but nothing Ralph does is documented so we are terrified of losing him. Ralph is overweight, smokes and never exercises. But he does whine a lot.

Under-employment is so severe [*pre-2009*] that the IT industry will give anyone a go based on there being something in their CV. In doing so, we often make mistakes:

- Past roles have little relevance to the proposed position: it is only the technology that is the same.

- Technology counts for too much. People and process skills are at least equally important in selecting an employee. Maybe they are an expert in CICS but if they can't manage their own diary and they alienate anyone unfortunate enough to work with them, then it might be better to train someone else in the technology.

- Formal qualifications are given little respect. Any qualification is good, and there are no minimum standards. Many qualifications are from institutions nobody has heard of. There are few standards for qualifications.

- The majority of "computer science" qualifications are irrelevant to the practical application of technology in business, especially older qualifications.

- Certifications with greater relevance often involve days or at most weeks of learning, are purely theoretical, and are tested only by written exam, often multi-choice. There are no apprenticeships, no internships, and no practical tests of capability.

- Experience is given too much weight. Simply doing time does not make an expert.

- Conversely, genuine experience can not be given enough weight. Just because someone "worked with" a technology does not measure their understanding of its practical application.

- The deepest we go into someone's past is reference checking, and often that is cursory or absent. There is little ongoing professional certification, and there are no registration bodies. People's careers are not recorded except in their CVs [hah!] and they are not subject to peer scrutiny.

IT is in a state of war and is running short of troops. Anyone fit enough to walk is given a gun and pushed over the top. That might work in trench warfare but it does not work in creating or managing complex technology. We wouldn't entrust Joe to build a multi-million-dollar bridge but in IT we regularly trust similarly unqualified inexperienced people to build equally expensive, equally mission-critical (and sometimes equally life threatening) systems. No wonder IT has such a woeful track record for project delivery and service levels.

The success of mediocrity in IT

The IT industry is a settling pond for mediocrity.

Here is a stereotype:

- IT worker: systems or network "engineer", support technician, programmer, vendor pre- or post-sales, consultant (well, contractor really). The older ones are architect, analyst, expensive consultant, or senior anything.
- No formal IT qualification/certification that took longer than a few days, or weeks at most. [A degree in computer science does not count: computer science is as relevant to business IT as chemistry is to mechanical engineering. Nor does any training count that everyone passes.]
- Changes employers on average every two or three years
- Nothing in the CV that relates to responsibility for any specific project delivered, just general "experience" with various technologies
- No references from direct reports and few from direct managers. Most turn out to be friends.
- "Accidental" entry to the IT industry:
    - worked as a clerk and started playing with the software, then got moved into IT;
    - a user poached by a vendor;
    - started at the loading dock: an operator or IT clerical worker who moved up;
    - nepotic appointment;
    - hired by a desperate company, straight out of college with a degree in something irrelevant
- Holds the IP keys to some key bit of technology that allows them to do very little most of the day
- Ducks accountability
- Prima donna expectations of their own importance
- You just know they are bluffing (let's not mess about: they are shovelling it) but they seldom get caught because no-one knows enough or monitors enough of what they do to be sure. They survive because their managers aren't smart enough or paying enough attention to spring them
- When the façade starts to crack they move on, with a CV now that much richer in "experience"

Here's another:

> Much the same background as above but they stay in one company producing very little business value, screwing up not quite often enough to be fired (after all where will we get a replacement?). They do a job for $70,000 p.a. that any smart college kid could learn in a solid month's training if someone could be bothered teaching them. The extreme example is Dilbert's colleague Wally.

Or another:

- IT line manager or "team leader" (same crap, less status, no extra privileges)
- Came up through the ranks from geek
- Management training consists solely of an in-house course with no examination or other verification of its effectiveness or the students' capability
- Inter-personal skills (Emotional Quotient) at the lower end of the scale
- Stressed, overworked and unhappy. Can't motivate staff and can't manage superiors.
- Says "yes" up and "no" down

Or another:

- Sales person: smart, personable, enthusiastic, driven
- Poached from a competitor, so they are busy for months spilling the beans about how the last company worked and what deals they were chasing
- Do everything asked of them, work hard
- Are out at clients a lot: usually only one contact per client, someone they get on with and visit constantly. Struggle to get access wider or higher in the decision tree
- Lots of prospects but struggle with qualified pipeline and seldom close anything [even a blind squirrel finds the occasional nut]
- There is always one big, high profile deal on the brink of closing

- They miss quota badly the first year but resolve to really go for it the second: talk their way into a second chance, usually based on the work invested in that one big deal
- As the second year draws to a close, they go to work for a competitor, who thinks they have pulled of a huge coup by poaching them

Take a look at those around you. At yourself. How often do any of those stereotypes come close?

IT leaves no hole: failed projects disappear in a puff of money. It is a complex, confusing, poorly measured industry. When people screw up, there is poor record keeping, measurement or accountability to nail the guilty, and a thick fog of shifting requirements, techno-babble and multiple consequences for those guilty to disappear behind.

There is no formal IT professionalism: there are no barriers to entry to the industry. Salaries are high - even the non-variable components of incentive-based schemes. As a consequence rogues, shysters, and snake oil salesmen thrive. They leap from job to job and people think they are successful. All they need is momentum and people think they are going somewhere.

Those deceived, or at least unable to correct the situation, are the IT managers. All this talk about aligning IT with the business demonstrates decades of business incompetence in IT managers. No-one talks about (re)-aligning Finance with the business, or HR. A majority of IT managers wouldn't survive a year in any other part of the organisation.

Last stereotype:
- CIO
- Came up through the ranks from geek. Stayed so long they got the top spot when the last one died.
- Struggles endlessly with their peer managers. No-one understands IT and IT is always failing to deliver.

- Reports to the CFO, or even one tier lower.
- Chronically short of money and staff

I met a different kind of CIO, one who talked hard–driving techno-babble that meant nothing. People who employed him figured that if they didn't understand, it meant he was brilliant.

His staff knew better but he bullied them into silence. He was big, dominating, intense, driven, and mentally unstable. He was stupid but had enough rat cunning to master the art of bluffing intelligence.

He ran IT at a major company for several years before his spectacular failure to deliver anything began to show. He quickly left and was on the speaking circuit and magazine covers for years as the ex-CIO. The ex-CIO title was just starting to get tired when he landed the national manager's job at a small vendor, where he can happily b.s. for years since his boss is overseas and few firms are as mismanaged, people-wise, as vendors.

The drivers of this phenomenon are

- Under-employment, under-employment and under-employment
- Inept IT management, unable to recognise or deal with the problem
- Inflated value given to "experience" with software. When they finally do leave, someone else usually steps in and learns enough to cope within a short time. It is not that hard, especially with the internet to help
- Absence of mechanisms to transfer IP within IT organisations: disciplined documentation of process, workflow automation, formal coaching programs, rotation of roles...
- No industry model for professional qualifications and apprenticeship [changing now, but it is still fragmented and immature]
- Hopeless tertiary education programs with minimal relevance to business IT
- Lack of professional bodies that are selective about who they take and expel those who don't continue to measure up
- The shroud of techno-confusion that IT throws up around itself to hide from the business

- Failure to check references

Picture the scene: ten tired, stressed vendor people in a room for four days, round the clock, building a proof of concept for a huge potential deal. The conference room is beige, windowless, stuffy, crackling with tension and smelling of pizza. The boss's mobile phone rings. He looks annoyed at the interruption, then his face brightens and he begins striding the room, obviously relishing the conversation: "Gillian? Yes, Gillian worked for me. What can I tell you about Gillian? Oh, I can't say enough about Gillian. She was without a doubt the laziest, most incompetent, inept employee it has ever been my misfortune to manage... Yes that's what I said. And then there was her inability to observe normal work hours and the endless sick days for mysterious... Listed me as a reference? That is illustrative of another of her qualities; stupidity, or possibly dishonesty. The reason I fired her... No wait don't go! There's so much more I could... Damn." Certainly relieved the tension, in fact we were in stitches. I'm sure Gillian never imagined they would actually check.

There is a light dawning. Signs appear that IT is growing up, readying itself to emerge as another branch of engineering, with standard measurable practices, professional standards and ongoing certification, and recognition of quality.

We can hope that the new millennium (this one) will drive the cowboys out of the industry and introduce enough rigour and maturity to make IT as exciting as mechanical engineering. But that is another discussion...

The rise of IT professionalism

There have always been professionals in our industry, sprinkled about like gold flakes in the mud. And other IT people have often meant well but been ill-equipped for the task.

And yes there have been those who exploited the immaturity of the system: the ethically- and motivationally-challenged who went for a ride. They blew their school years and they don't like to work hard, but they were blessed with brains. So they are smart enough to bluff their way in to the high-paying positions of our industry.

However a sea change is underway in the IT industry. Leading the way are the project managers and system testers, who have had formal bodies of knowledge and accreditation for some time. Industry certifications like the British Certified IT Professional (CITP) are emerging, along with associated skills frameworks like the SFIA[1]. Now it is the ITSM practitioners with ITIL and ISO20000 accreditation and the first baby steps of professional organisations.

We still have a long way to go to meet the levels of best practice set by other industries. A professional is measured by three attributes: their attitude, development and ability.

Attitude

Why do dentists promote oral hygiene? A doctor wants to keep you alive as long as possible to maximise revenue, but why should a dentist care how you look after your teeth, other than to create a more pleasant work environment?

Because they are professionals. First and foremost a professional acts in the best interests of their customer, not themselves.

And why are dentists expensive? Cheap dentists are rare and don't stay around long, because customers want a quality job when

---

[1] http://www.sfia.org.uk/

someone is working inside their skull. The second attitude of professionals is a commitment to a quality result.

Actually, that is the third. The second attitude is commitment to a result. Professionals want to build something, want to see their work completed, and want to deliver an outcome to their customer/employer.

Finally professionals tend to be tidy. They cover all the details, tie up loose ends, and seek completeness.

Development

The term "engineer" is bandied about the IT industry at times but almost nobody in our industry is an engineer.

A real engineer has a tertiary qualification. They studied physics, chemistry, advanced mathematics, programming, CAD/drafting, mtal shop, first aid. They studied other branches of engineering as well as their own so that they understand the basics of electronics, mechanics, optics, geology, hydrology, and so on. They spent three or four years or more learning their trade, including practical experience. Many failed.

A real engineer doesn't come straight out of university and design a hydroelectric dam. They serve apprenticeship, working with senior engineers to prove their mettle.

Once they have enough experience and some good referees, engineers seek accreditation by their professional body. Only then are they a real engineer.

And if they screw up, or bring the profession into disrepute, they will lose that accreditation.

The engineering profession sets the benchmark for professional development. Engineers are entrusted with millions of dollars of other people's money in order to build complex systems. Many of these systems impact the well-being and safety of the public. Most of them are critical in some way to an organisation, and they either work or they don't. Sound familiar? The difference is that engineers' mistakes stand as a rusting monument to their incompetence, whereas IT mistakes leave no crater.

Ability

The best way to assess someone's ability is to ask their peers. The best way to do that is via professional accreditation but we still do not have a lot of that in the IT industry. The worst way to assess is to ask the person, but if all else fails you can look at that great work of fiction - their CV.

We should not settle for any less professionalism (attitude, development and proven ability) in the person we entrust with a multi-million-dollar IT project than we expect in the person who is responsible for the steel beam to hold up the foyer roof, or the electrical system that runs through the building, or the train we ride to work.

Yet we do. IT has an alarming propensity for giving anyone a go. The standards will not rise until the consumers of IT services demand it. So look for professionals.

How to find a professional

Professionalism shows outwardly in a person's presentation. Boffins, geeks and geniuses might be vague and rumpled, but professionals aren't. Professionals are tidy, orderly, literate, self-confident. They have good interpersonal skills. So make sure you interview candidates in person. Ask them to write something and to present it.

If you are stuck with the CV as the only evidence of their ability, examine what they did personally. People who have "three years experience with Novell networks" or "worked as a systems engineer" have not done anything. Find out what projects they were personally responsible for – what they delivered. Ask tough questions to probe as to what the outcomes were. Beware of a pattern of leaving before the project ended. Real professionals want to see the conclusion. Check references.

Give preference to professional accreditation where it exists. Call for and encourage new professional bodies. Push for change.

The new professionalism

The situation is changing. Organisation such as PMI (Project Management Institute), national Computer Societies, and others are offering accreditation. Occasionally a university offers a degree that means something useful to the industry. The industry is attracting more professional people.

We have a very long way to go to match the standards of engineers and doctors. There needs to be international standards of tertiary qualification, and very different courses offered by the universities. There needs to be international networks of accreditation. Most of all there must be much higher expectations set of the people we entrust with these huge projects.

What shall we call IT professionals? Personally I like Information Engineer. But lock that name up in legislation just as other professions have done, otherwise everyone in IT will have it on their business card as next year's replacement for "Senior Consultant".

Information engineering

When we speak of a new profession(alism), could it be that by focusing on IT we are focusing on the wrong thing?

My other interest besides being a nuisance is railroads. I just read the line "railroads nurtured the new profession of civil engineering in the 19th Century" (...in America. It's one of those "the world ends at the shining seas" books[1].) This resonated with me. Can we paraphrase to "Information Technology nurtured the new profession of"... WHAT?

We - or at least I am always on about the profession of IT, or I prefer "Information Engineering". But maybe the real profession isn't about information any more than civil engineering is about railroads. Maybe the profession is about building complex people systems, about - dare I say it - process, and of course the cultural change to introduce/refine/grow that process.

I put it to the audience that the information age, digital technology, and the internet, (and probably some more factors like the rise of the corporation), have all combined to lift people-process to a new level of complexity, just like railroads forced civil engineering to new levels by the railroad's demand for gentle curves and gradients.

The real profession that we see emerging or maturing is.... what?

> Systems engineer? (And not as we meant it when that was a trendy IT title)
>
> Process engineer?
>
> Or is Information Engineer a good description anyway?
>
> Or something else...

---

[1] *Landmarks on the Iron Road*, W. Middleton, Indiana University Press 1999, ISBN-13: 978-0253335593

Historically bridges were always the big driving force for civil engineering, but up until the 19th Century most of them were made by people who had little idea what they were doing. They had no scientific basis for it. They just used gut feel, guesswork and copying to build their bridges. The most experienced built the best bridges, but some still fell down and nobody exactly knew why. Sound familiar?

The industrial revolution changed that. Suddenly canal aqueducts and later railroad bridges were required that had to carry enormously higher loads while staying nice and level and steady. And they were much much longer and higher: with a road you can dip down into the valley as far as possible, have a nice short bridge, and then crawl back up the other side. Not so with canals or trains. Lastly, when double-heading steam locos thunder onto a bridge at 60 mph, believe me you need a whole new order of engineering. Along with that came tunnels and cuttings and fills on a scale never conceived of before.

And it wasn't just the design that changed. It was the logistics of building on such a larger scale. When my Dad ran a data centre, there was 64k of memory. It basically added up the day's cheques and deposits for the banks, and spewed out a bunch of totals. These days ERP and CRM and the Windows desktop is a whole different ballgame.

Also in *Landmarks on the Iron Road* on page 4

In the decade between 1870 and 1880 railroad and highway bridges collapsed at a rate of about forty a year [in the USA]... Frequently, designers had an imperfect understanding of the forces... or of the potential dangers... Steadily increasing loads often subjected bridges to stresses for which they had never been designed... All too commonly bridges were hastily built by the cheapest means... Quite generally, too, bridges were designed and built for the railroads by independent bridge companies on a competitive bid basis.

Woooooo spooky.

IT exists to manage the flow of data, in the same way that railroads exist to manage the flow of freight and passengers.

My point is that the professionals who built railroads weren't railroaders. They also built for canals and, later, for freeways and pipelines and airports and...

At a layer of abstraction removed from IT there is a profession emerging that builds complex people systems, of which IT is currently the major enabler just as railroads were the only engineering game in town in 1880.

Personal development

What shape are you?

How you configure your knowledge shape has a major effect on your employment and career prospects.

"Knowledge shape"? We are talking about your profile or portfolio of knowledge and skills. Profiles or shapes can range across the spectrum from generalist to specialist or expert, from broad and shallow to narrow and deep, from jack-of-all-trades to master-of-one. (See some tongue-in-cheek examples in the illustrations on the next pages).

The trend within IT is to respect the specialist, to automatically aspire to deep expertise as a career objective. Not so fast.

The choices you make for your knowledge shape can affect the jobs you get, the value you deliver within those jobs and your job satisfaction.

One of the basic traps of technical careers is the expert cul-de-sac. Once you are the guru, you tend to get stuck there. The company does not want you to move on because nobody else can do it better. The narrower your expertise, the fewer are your options in the organisation or elsewhere. You can be overqualified, or not a good fit. Once you reach the pinnacle of your field, you have to go down again before you can ascend.

Sometimes your area of specialisation can start to melt away as technology changes. You end up like a polar bear on an ice floe, with a tough swim ahead of you once it disappears. I learned this lesson early by becoming a world expert in a proprietary mainframe fourth-generation language. Good career move that one... not.

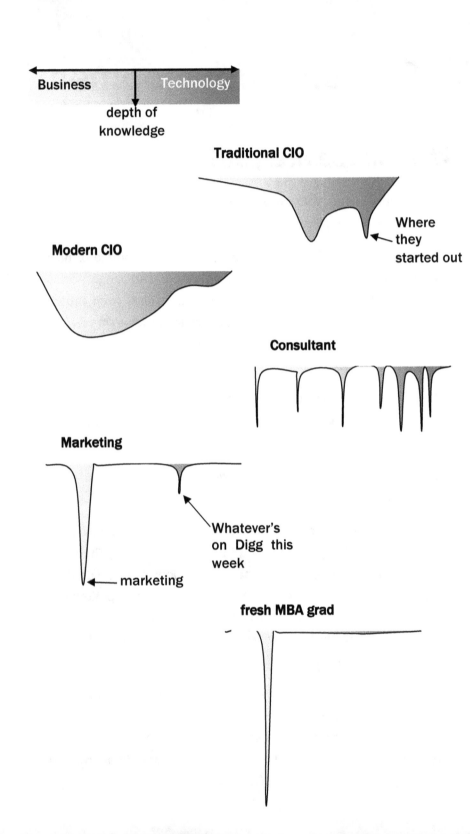

Solutions Architect

Geek

Business Analyst

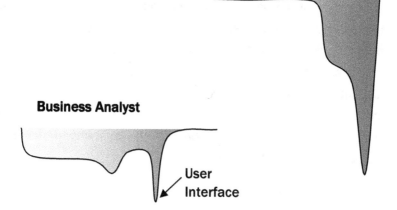

User
Interface

Architect

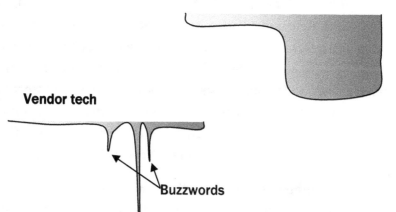

Vendor tech

Buzzwords

Those who escape the expert cul-de-sac often go into architecture or business technologist or business analyst, but these roles are generalist roles. The shift is difficult. It requires an exceptional person who can be both broad and deep. Or it requires learning multiple new areas and unlearning one, to morph your knowledge shape. It is possible to un-learn, but only somewhat. You can take the boy out of the technology but you can't completely take the technology out of the boy (or girrrl). It hurts to abandon expertise. It is like surgical removal. It particularly hurts if you must give up technical areas altogether to learn your business, or to learn new disciplines like warehousing, writing, finance, marketing, communications, politics, analysis or people management. We get withdrawal symptoms. I dealt with them by furtively building a spreadsheet now and then with unnecessary features. When I formed my own company, I implemented my own LAMP stack and CMS for the new business servers, because it was a sound business decision to do it myself (Yeah right!).

Deep expertise is not necessarily a disadvantage in job hunting. When the right job comes up you won't face much competition. At times you will be headhunted. Sometimes you can name your price. For as long as your expertise matters, your boss will love you... and cut you some slack. Over twenty years ago the IBM expert on these new-fangled machines called ATMs arrived in Australia. Among the standard IBM suits and haircuts he dressed in t-shirt and jeans, had a beard and long hair. The reaction of the bank executives he came to meet? "Man he must be good". For the cynics among you (and there are a few in IT), specialists can wedge themselves firmly in a niche where they go unnoticed for periods of time, and get to play with some serious toys. Be warned: there is danger of complacency here that we discussed in How Secure is Your IT Technical Career?

The final advantage of deep expertise: it feels good to master any domain, you can deliver to almost any requirement within your space, and there is great satisfaction (and ego-food) in being Da

Man (or Woman): the oracle (small "O") with a path beaten to your door.

This article is not saying expertise is bad. Just don't let it be your assumed course without considering the options in the light of what is going on in your organisation and the industry, and of where you want to be in ten or twenty years. Just as there are jobs suited to a deep knowledge of a narrow band, there are as many that require multi-faceted skills. The generalist probably has more employment options, though more competition for them.

As you will have gathered, I made the shift from specialist to generalist years ago. For me personally it is about problem solving. If I am to deliver solutions to employer or client, I need to be well rounded (those who know me will vouch that is true at least physically). Synthesis from multiple strands is what I enjoy, and at the time there was a crying need for technical generalists at my employer firm. So I was able to differentiate strongly, change career direction (which was veering into management – yech), and increase my value (read: pay). Taking the cynical view again, generalists tend to advise and guide while accountability and the messy business of delivering fall to the specialists. While generalists are often busy that does not mean they are necessarily doing much.

Seriously, the generalist role can be rewarding to employer and employee. With too many specialists, nobody straddles the problem, and nobody bridges between groups, especially between IT and the business. It is the big picture person who sets the direction, shapes the overall solution, and brings everyone together, while the specialists get the job done. Can a foreigner like me say that specialists are East Coast and generalists are West Coast USA?

So take some time to think about what knowledge shape you are now, and what shape you need to be to get where you want to be. It can make all the difference.

So you want to be a consultant

IT as an industry and especially IT today, is well suited to a career as a consultant. To those who are not consultants the grass can look very green, and the job can look pretty easy. As we will see it is not, but for those with the right qualities and skills consulting is indeed a lucrative career option.

Consulting appeals to those who want to make a difference, or who want independence or more money. Or all of the above.

For the purposes of this article we consider independent consulting, but most of the article applies equally to those who prefer to stay safely in the embrace of paid employment as a consultant for a company (always known on business cards as a "Senior" or "Principal" Consultant).

Mostly though, consulting offers the dream of breaking free, of ttjasi (telling them to Take This Job and Shove It). And it delivers that, to those suited to it.

The IT industry has several attributes that make it attractive to work for yourself:

- Shortage of skilled people – a seller's market [*pre-2009*]. There are high overall levels of under-employment (vacancies) in the IT industry. There are also many specialist niches where experience in some esoteric technology or process gives you a unique business value. Some of these niches are generated by new trends, e.g. Web 2.0 developer or ITIL Change Manager, and others by the opposite process – the aging workforce and legacy technologies, e.g. Cobol programmer or CICS systems programmer.

- This shortage leads to high hourly rates of pay. On contract you can make in a few months what the average full-time worker earns in a year. You can either make a lot of money or take a lot of time off, depending on your approach and priorities.

- Low requirements for qualification or certification. To build a bridge you must have the appropriate engineering registration, which in turn requires qualification, certification, experience and recognition. In IT we will give anyone a go. A piece of paper helps sometimes, but experience counts for much more. Even experience is not essential, so long as you have the chutzpah to stand up and say you know the way.

- High levels of on-the-job training by employers. Compared to other industries, IT employers of full-time staff are willing to pay for a lot of training. If training is useful or certification is desirable for your planned consulting career, it is often possible to get all the training you need while still in fulltime employment.

- High levels of change, especially projects. Consulting thrives on change. Change introduces uncertainty and people look for answers. Change introduces peaks in workload, so temporary additional resources are required. And projects release funds, which consultants are happy to mop up.

As a result anyone working in IT is usually well paid and has useful knowledge, which puts us in good shape to consider self-employment. Whatever you choose to do, you need three assets:

- A strong financial position. There may well be a dip in income as you establish yourself. And there is always the risk, however small, that it just won't work. IT people tend to have lower debt levels and more financial reserves to help justify the risk and weather the initial impact.

- A unique business value: an uncommon area of knowledge and experience.

- Basic business knowledge. You now run a business, so you have to be able to cope with accounting, cash-flow, record-keeping and compliance.

There are a number of options open to you to work for yourself in IT. Ignoring some of the more esoteric ones such as developing a software product or launching a website or writing, there are two main sectors; consulting and contracting. People often confuse the two because consultants usually work to contracts.

In the generally understood IT usage of "contractor", this is someone who provides labour on contract, to fill a role that would otherwise require a full-time employee to do it, either because a full-timer cannot be found, or there is a short term requirement, or management are hiding the headcount in op-ex.

You can do very well as a contractor of you have a skill that is in short supply. A friend of mine went into a DBA position for three months at a small regional bank running an unusual mainframe database. He was still on contract rates a decade later (though they often begged him to go full-time). Eventually the party ended when the bank finally got swallowed and the systems absorbed, but by then he was all set for retirement.

"Consultants" on the other hand sell information not labour. They draw on intellectual property that the organization does not have in order to provide planning, advice, opinion or review.

(To go back to fulltime employed consultants for a moment, "consultant" is often misused by large firms to refer to "engineer" or even "technician". Consultants don't build things and they don't fix things. The lines are blurred of course, but the word "consultant" appears on the business card of many who most clearly are not.)

Consulting is an altogether different game to contracting, and it requires a greater skill-set. In addition to some intellectual property that differentiates you, you also need to be good at many or all of the following:

- Communication. Only some IT people know how to write a recommendation paper, to facilitate a meeting/workshop, to explain themselves clearly, to frame an email to get the desired result. Given that IT people tend to be well above average intelligence, this common weakness used to mystify me. I think now that it comes because of the lack of formal qualification. Smart people who never went to university can carve a path for themselves anyways in IT, but they do not learn these essential skills. Either that or it is a condemnation of our education systems. Come to think of it that is probably closer to the mark.

- Gathering Knowledge. Even fewer people know how to research, to interview and investigate, to organize information, to abstract and summarize. For why this might be, see "Communication".

- Politics. And very few IT people indeed know how to play the game, to read the political winds, to understand power, to influence results. One of my best business teachers, Art Jacobs, said there are three kinds of people: an inner circle who makes things happen by playing politics, a ring around them of people who choose not to participate but make sure they watch what is happening, and an outer group who exclaim "what the **** happened?". That outer group is very large in IT. Effective consultants can survive in the second ring but the real shakers and movers get into that inner circle.

- Common sense. From some of the outputs we see from consultants, it seems this is not essential, or common. But the really good consultants have the ability to cut to the chase, identify the basic issues, and come up with workable pragmatic ideas or solutions without being purists or impossible dreamers.

- Work ethic. Good consultants work hard, like to set things right, pay attention to detail, and stick at it until they get a result.

- Relationships. Consultants have to use networks, gain trust, get agreement and support, make people do things, and change minds. IT is full of misanthropes who prefer not to interact with fellow humans. This is great because it makes good consultants scarce.

Assuming you have got this far, there are some specialized skills required as a consultant - the tools of the trade. Ensure you already have most of the following skills, or go out and acquire them:

- Selling. Even with the current shortages, work does not just jump in the door. You must generate pipeline, follow up leads, and close deals. The product you are selling is yourself, so know how to do this: market yourself, present yourself well, instil confidence, and look for opportunities.

- Cultural change. Much of what consultants do is effecting change. There is a formal body of knowledge around how you do this, and recognized techniques for making it happen.

- Teaching. Most people think they are good at passing concepts to other adults. Most are awful. Learn how to teach adults properly.

- Specialized consulting techniques. There are dozens of techniques for facilitating, analysis, problem solving and other consulting activities. These include root cause analysis, causal chain, cause and effect, fishbone diagrams, why-how maps, Pareto charts, Boston matrix, Kepner-Tregoe, six serving men, affinity diagrams, clustering, rich pictures, force field analysis, Mind Mapping, spider diagrams, SCOTSMAN, SWOT/PEST, hurdling and ranking, voting, weighting, sorting by importance, brainstorming, nominal group, Six Thinking Hats ...

If you have the foundation abilities in communication, politics, and so on, and you have acquired the specialist skills for the consultant's tool bag, then you can sally forth to make a difference for your clients and make money along the way.

Profiling

Profiling is the art of guessing what kind of person you are dealing with: what they like, and how they want you to interact with them. If you can "read" people effectively, you can modify your own style and approach to best suit the way *they* want to proceed. This will greatly increase your chances of getting the outcome you desire.

This may smack of that sordid business called selling. It is a very powerful sales technique, but we all sell in other ways, every day: asking your boss for something; joining a project team; persuading a workmate; explaining a purchase to a spouse. If your style is miss-matched to their preference, it will grate. You risk annoying them and failing to communicate effectively. So everybody should understand something about profiling.

There are two kinds of people: those who divide people into two groups and those who don't. Me, I'm one of the latter: I divide people into four groups. For day to day encounters with people, it is very effective to quickly classify them into one of four groups in order to determine the best way to interact with them. Much as I am a fan of the Rule of threes – people like to understand three of anything – in the case of people, three is not enough. To usefully categorise people, you need four. I can hear the howls of protest now; "you can't lump the endless variation of the human race into four groups – people cannot be pigeon-holed, and especially not into so few categories".

Well, you can. Try it. It is imperfect and sometimes difficult, but it can also be startlingly effective.

As to what four categories to use, that doesn't actually matter that much so long as you have a model that works for you, and some predetermined rules for how you will respond to each of the four categories.

It is all Jung's fault. Dr. Carl Jung started it with Feeler, Sensor, Thinker and Intuituve. The majority of other systems stem from this.

A well-known four-way categorisation is DISC® Profiling. DISC goes further than just putting people into four buckets but at its heart there are four main types of people, arranged in the model as four quadrants.

Wikipedia says:

> DISC is an acronym for:
>
> Dominance - relating to control, power and assertiveness
>
> Influence - relating to social situations and communication
>
> Steadiness (submission in Marston's time)- relating to patience, persistence, and thoughtfulness
>
> Conscientiousness (or caution, compliance in Marston's time) - relating to structure and organization
>
> These four dimensions can be grouped in a grid with D and I sharing the top row and representing extroverted aspects of the personality, and C and S below representing introverted aspects. D and C then share the left column and represent task-focused aspects, and I and S share the right column and represent social aspects. In this matrix, the vertical dimension represents a factor of "Assertive" or "Passive", while the horizontal represents "Open" vs. "Guarded".

DISC allows you to look at someone's environment that they surround themselves with, listen to them speak, watch them behave, and then categorise them in order to predict their preferred mode of behaviour from you. At least, that is how I use it. It results in some very crude simplifications, but it works for me. "He's high I: better encourage him to talk about himself for a while. Make sure I show what's in it for him". "She's an S: I'll need to get a few more team-members on side first". "He's a C: don't rush him - settle in for a long and detailed discussion of every bit of information I have with me". If you want to be able to walk into a stranger's office and quickly think "Oops she's a high D – better present the facts as quickly and orderly as possible then cut to the chase" then get yourself some DISC training.

But the really interesting thing is that it does not have to be DISC.

There is a very similar four-colour system - red green, yellow, blue – whose origins I'm not sure of.

My greatest teacher, Art Jacobs, created a categorisation system in the earlier versions of Target Account Selling (TAS) which classified IT people by what motivates them: money, technology, relationships or business. So – crudely - you know whether to sell to them on price, features, trust or ROI. That model has worked well for me too.

I also like the Situational Leadership model (Hersey, Blanchard & Johnson, *Management of Organizational Behavior*, 9th edition 2008) that modifies your style of leadership based on the employee's readiness or maturity: from Directing through Coaching to Supporting and finally Delegating. While on the surface it categorises the leader's style, it is all about selecting one of the four styles by profiling the employee.

Probably the best known profiling system of any sort is Myers Briggs, or more precisely the Myers-Briggs Type Indicator® (MBTI) "personality inventory". The basis of MBTI is two four-way models, which are combined to produce 16 possible categorisations of people. This is very powerful for working out group dynamics, where you have the luxury of a day to workshop what your profile is and how to relate to your team-mates.

But I'm wary of people who say they can meet someone and quickly determine that they are INTJ. Certainly I cannot deal with 16 levels of categorisation while meeting someone for the first time, or trying to predict the response of someone who I have met twice. Four is enough.

Incidentally, the Myers-Briggs results can be spookily accurate – once you get to a granularity of 16 the fit can almost be too close for comfort. Mind you, sometimes astrological profiles sound like a good fit too, and every bone of my scientific being tells me they are crap. So I do approach Myers-Briggs sceptically. It lacks any rigorous scientific background, but it seems to work. The same is true of just about all models for classifying people; they arise from someone's insight not from scientific measurement.

And if they work for you, that is all that matters. That is what they are for. It doesn't matter if some of the time you can't get a good match, and other times you are wrong, so long as fairly often you can modify your own behaviour successfully to get the result you need from someone else.

So find one or more profiling classification models that you are comfortable with. Learn how to quickly categorise people. Work out which category you are in. Learn the rules for how your type should interact with the others. Especially know what not to do, or what to do to avoid potential difficulties. Then apply the rules and see for yourself how useful they are.

The alternative is to charge in and just be yourself. Often enough this will be wrong for them. If four really is the magic number for categorising people, then you'll get it wrong about three times in four. With profiling, you might do better than fifty/fifty.

Management Management

There is much attention paid to processes these days in IT, with Operations Management, Change Management, and a raft of Something Managements. Perhaps the most important thing to manage is seldom mentioned: your boss.

Managing your manager is as important an activity as the function you are employed for, or managing your personal finances or your household. It should receive the same thought and effort.

Without Management Management, you have no control over the most important influence on your career; your boss. They write your reviews, set your pay, assign you work, decide your moves and your leave. Without Management Management you are at the whim of that person. Think about that. It is seldom an attractive prospect (and you are very lucky if it is attractive).

The process of Management Management involves three strategic goals: look after yourself, look after your boss, and look after the organisation.

Look after yourself

In my work, I found many who had no awareness of their own situation and no plan or actions to protect and develop their career. Work is work: your first priority is to yourself and your family or other dependents. There has been any number of books and articles about putting yourself first, about work/life balance, about working to live not living to work. This is not the place to re-visit all that, but in the context of Management Management the main reasons we manage our manager are to protect that work/life balance and to nurture our career.

In order to look after yourself, the first step is to understand your boss: their KPIs (what is it they are measured on and answerable for?), what drives them (why do they come to work?), what turns them on (in a work context of course). Also understand the context within which they operate: what the business is doing, what it wants, where they fit, what threats there are to you and to them. Develop some "corporate situational awareness":

- what are the strategies of your organisation, both the official ones and the real ones

- what changes are coming, or are likely to be coming

- who is really in power, locally and at the top

- who are in the inner circles

Second step is to make sure you are seen - don't hide your light. Technical people are appallingly bad at this, at least in the cultures I know. Don't expect the formal processes to automatically generate recognition for you. Don't expect your boss to do research to learn how clever and useful (and profitable) you are. When you do something good, tell someone. Tell everyone. Practice doing this humbly, discretely, but practice making sure people know. Especially your boss.

Third step is to let your boss know what you need. Don't expect them to guess or find out (or care). If you can frame a deal, all the better: find a win-win, something in it for you and your boss. If you need something and there is no quid pro quo for your boss or the organisation, it will hardly be a high priority. Make it explicit (don't leave things implied, don't be circumspect) and remind them occasionally (without being annoying).

Once you have practices in place to be aware of your environment – especially your boss, to make others aware of you, and to communicate your needs to your boss, then you are ready to work towards the second goal...

Look after your manager

Give them what they want. You might have your own ideas about what is important and what the priorities should be, but consider who is paying you and what they are paying you for. If they are paying you to set the priorities then you probably don't need this article. If setting priorities is in your job description, good for you. If it isn't, better you work to your boss's priorities not yours.

When it comes to review time and pay-setting time and promotion time, the person who gave most to the boss will be the one at the front of your boss's mind. There are three ways to deliver to them: help deliver their KPIs, take away (or prevent) some pain, or make them look good.

If you have worked on the first goal well, you will know what your boss needs to deliver to their boss. If their number one KPI[1] is to get a certain project in by end of year, or to cut costs by 10%, and you serve that up to them, it will never be forgotten.

A related deliverable is to realise what bugs them and make it better. Don't make the mistake of thinking this is just as good as delivering on a KPI – it isn't. But pulling a thorn will win points.

Don't be precious about credit or glory – le them have it. They know they owe you.

Pay attention to their safety. Stop them doing the wrong thing: move sharp objects out of the way, redirect them. This is most effective if you can make it their idea.

Note what is not on this list: delivering to your own KPIs. That is just expected. If you do, you have done no more than your job. Your boss will like it but not particularly notice it.

---

[1] Key Performance Indicator: number-based goal or target.

People will say this is too Dilbertesque: that not all bosses are pointy-haired idiots. Indeed they are not, but what we are describing here is simple human nature. Even the nicest, most caring, most enlightened boss cannot help but subconsciously favour the person who made their job easier.

Besides, there are way more manager's positions than there are good managers.

Look after your organisation

Management Management may manipulate... um manage your boss to protect your own interests, but those interests must also align (to some extent) with the interests of the organisation. The more they don't, the more you travel into areas which are ethically or legally questionable.

Secondly, as you work with your boss you have a responsibility to look at their actions that are not initiated or encouraged by you but nevertheless you are aware of them or a party to them. Is your boss doing what is good for the entity? At some point you have a responsibility to escalate an alert, but first try to redirect them as above.

Connect to your manager

Accept the reality: your manager is seldom going to come to you. You share their attention with how many other direct reports? Add in their peers, their boss and their customers and you can see you have to go get attention.

For a small number of you, you get on well with your manager as human beings: you have a friendly relationship. For the rest, in order to engage with your manager you may need to study up on communication models – how to connect.

There are several systems to better understand how to relate by profiling your manager (see Profiling). Take your pick from DISC®, Herrmann Brain Dominance Instrument®, personality colours (red, green, yellow and blue), or Myers-Briggs amongst others.

Also study up on situational leadership. This has four modes of interaction: directing, coaching, supporting, delegating. Which mode is your boss in when dealing with you, and where do you want them to be? If there is a mismatch you can talk to them about it, and/or try to manage them into your preferred mode.

Developing your negotiation skills won't hurt either.

And finally steep yourself in business understanding and language. I did it by subscribing to the Economist and the McKinsey Quarterly for several years.

There are those who see this as sucking up. If you see your role to be one where you do not co-operate with your boss, or you actively work against them, then you are in the wrong job. You are employed to be an effective agent of the organisation. For good or ill the organisation has decided that your boss is the one to direct you in that. Your goal should be to maximise the personal benefit of working for the organisation whilst also meeting the needs of that organisation. That benefit will be best when your boss sees you as their most valued employee.

You can change the system and you can work around your boss. But you will be more effective if you can manage your boss than if you are their biggest problem.

Managing Technical People

Managing what you can't measure

"You can't manage what you can't measure". Who on earth came up with that one? One of my big concerns about the application of process frameworks such as ITIL[1] is the emphasis on KPIs. Useful but dangerous.

Management is about the operation of a function or process. Even though I bet somewhere we have sanitary disposal managers these days, back in the real world "manager" means someone who manages people. They build processes around people and they make them follow those processes but at the end of the day managers manage people.

And you can't measure people. Oh, we try. But you can't. Einstein got unimpressive grades. So many modern corporate ills stem from managers trying to manage people by numbers.

First, I have seen brilliant people (read: valuable corporate resources) laid off because the numbers fingered them. Bad managers applying bad numbers.

Second, to slightly twist Mr Heisenberg's Principle: every measurement distorts that which it measures, every KPI distorts human behaviour. No KPI perfectly reflects the desired outcome - it always leads the measured subjects off the desired path.

---

[1] ITIL is a bunch of process documentation for IT operations. It is wildly popular right now. You don't need to know a thing about ITIL to follow this article.

Management by measurement leads to some weird results (every civil service is awash with them).

Third, the KPI hasn't been invented that measures "good". I used to have to rank my staff, 1 to 12, no equals. What a nonsense. The ranking would shift from day to day depending on the challenges the team faced. It would change from hour to hour depending on who had pissed me off last (just kidding).

Management by measurement is only a substitute for inept management. Put another way, it is an organisation's compensation for its inability to attract, create and retain good managers. Any decent manager can make correct assessment of staff based on instinct and subjective observation. Numbers help, and they particularly help fire someone, but you can manage what you can't measure. Good managers do it every day.

Metrics are for managing the "task environment". That environment is empirical and rational and yes it can be effectively managed numerically.

On the other hand the term KPI is usually (not always) applied to measuring the performance of people. This is what I object to, when it becomes slavish. Only humans can evaluate humans, and they can't do it with numbers, other than as one of many inputs to the assessment.

Managers manage both the task environment and the people in it. The skills and techniques of one don't work for the other.

A manager enacts change and an administrator makes it so. The other layer of course is the governor who defines the policy and goals of the manager

I have done a lot of work on professional development of staff. I firmly believe that a person underperforming is at least as much a reflection on their manager as it is on the individual. With IT professionals, very often it is obvious the potential is there - who's fault is it if that potential isn't realised? It is the manager's job to bring it out. If the metrics are bad, the boss also has some explaining to do.

Churn is a good indicator of a manager. People join jobs. They leave managers.

A comment on the IT Skeptic blog said:.

> "You can't measure people." However, you certainly can measure whether they do what is expected of them, you certainly can measure their performance against standards, and you also can measure their relative performance against their co-workers.

"You can't measure people but you can measure people"? You'll need stronger reasoning than that. My whole argument is that measures exist, and are used excessively by inept managers who can't deal with real live people without putting numbers in the way (not that I'm for a moment suggesting you're an inept manager), but that in and of themselves numbers don't measure people.

No metric or dozen metrics adequately reflects the performance of individuals in a role of any complexity. That sort of time-and-motion thinking might work for unskilled workers in an old-world industrial task, but in modern service industries all but the most basic of roles such as call-centre operator or data entry clerk have too many aspects and subtleties for numbers to fairly and truly reflect an employee's contribution. You can't measure any of those things listed: you can't measure whether they do what is expected of them, you can't measure their performance against standards, and you can't measure their relative performance against their co-workers.

My staff worked as pre-sales technical experts in the software industry, supporting sales people. They had no regular output product of their own; they engaged in entirely different transactions every time; they added value in complex, subtle and often unnoticed ways; and they functioned as part of a complex team with no individual accountability for the outcome. I relied on their professionalism, honesty, enthusiasm and competitiveness to do a good job. How do we measure those? And how do we measure them in such a way that the metric doesn't over-simplify the situation and therefore distort the behaviour? All metrics do.

And how do we compare staff in such a way that you can say that overall this person is "better" than this one? How do we objectively rank staff without using those same distortive, over-simplifying metrics? Nobody is better or worse than anyone else on paper. When the call comes from above to lay off one of them because it is time for the corporation to demonstrate its loyalty to its most valued resources once again, the decision ought to be made looking forward based on an infinitely complex web of anticipated requirements from the business and estimated future potentials of the staff, not on some arbitrary numbers that reflect one sad little side of the past story.

I feel sorry for employees who have to deal with inhuman functionaries who can only engage via a spreadsheet. I'm proud that I dealt with my staff as people not resources. Oh, I had spreadsheets and metrics, and I used them as I should have: as one more source of information to use when deciding the fate of friends and colleagues who deserve better than being treated as cogs in the machine.

Good managers don't manage by numbers, and bad managers misuse numbers.

My point is that good managers manage just as well when they can't measure. (And many things that matter - like people - can't be measured). Therefore the statement "you can't manage what you can't measure" is B.S.

Coping with Geeks

Hopefully most readers will agree that people working in IT can broadly be categorised into two groups: those who are oriented around action (process, business, projects) and those who are oriented about things (hardware and software technology, documents, data, content). The term geek has already been attached to the latter group, so while it is not universally viewed as a positive term, we use it here to describe the people within IT who are more interested in the technology than the procedures and strategies and business drivers to use it.

Because of this group's orientation, they lack respect for many of the imperatives that matter to the business (to varying degrees of course, depending on the individual). In the extreme this is manifest as undisguised contempt for the sordid business of making money, derision of project managers' obsession with time and completeness, and disgust with management's pragmatic compromises and expediencies. To the geek mind only the technology is important, and there is only one way to implement it: the correct way.

Those who run the business tend to be much more from the action-oriented group. They lack affinity for technology so they need the geeks, but they get frustrated by sloppy procedures, slipped deadlines, tactless communications, mystifying documents, warped priorities, lack of respect, non-compliance and stubborn resistance. Geeks just don't get it.

This is indeed a stereotyping generalisation, but a real one. I interviewed a Unix systems programmer in a bank once about the machines he "owned". I asked him what applications ran on them. He started listing HP-UX, Oracle, OpenView... No, I said, *applications*; what business processes? He looked surprised and just slightly embarrassed, because he had no idea.

For the health of the business it is most important that management understand the different mentality and manage appropriately. This is a huge topic beyond the scope of one article. Please do make a study of it as effective geek-management rewards the effort. In the meantime we can help by pointing out the most important threats to watch out for that can arise from geek culture.

Assessment of risk. Geeks tend to underestimate risk outside of their technical domain because they are dismissive of all but the components that matter to them. Make sure assurances that it will be alright are backed up with some evidence. Get a second opinion.

Return on investment. This may not even be considered in a request. Geeks think the company should spend whatever it takes to achieve a technically perfect outcome. Get architects or business technologists to translate geek-speak and evaluate the business benefits.

Compliance with policy, rules and standards. Geeks don't like bureaucracy, and they don't like dotting "I"s and crossing "T"s except when comparing technical specs. Get someone else to make sure it meets all the non-technical requirements.

Business impact. To geeks, the business is an abstract entity "out there" that does not understand what is important, nor the burdens they have to bear. Implement change control over infrastructure and have a non-geek review and approve the timing and implications of changes.

People. Known to geeks as "wetware", people are perceived as a major impediment to their effective functioning, second only to security. Buffer end users from geeks with a Service Desk. Invite geeks to meetings only when you have to. Don't expect them to wear silly hats or go abseiling or other "team" activities. And don't let them near...

Management. Geeks make bad people managers. Do not allow them to ascend by sheer force of seniority into management or even team leading roles. Even worse, do not commit the cardinal sin of pushing them into management roles they do not want (usually through lack of other career paths). Sometimes geeks experience a 'road to Damascus' revelation and suddenly begin to understand the other half (the author puts himself in this group). Most don't.

Project management. Geeks make bad project managers. Recall they are thing- not action-oriented. They do what they must to get it done. The actual doing is an ordeal to be endured and minimised. Only the essentials matter, but the technical essentials must be done right: they can't be rushed. Coordinating other people, ensuring all the bases are covered and everything fits together, driving for deadlines, coping with adversity, expedient adjustment, keeping records, reporting and analysing – these are not geek skills. PMs are a specialised group of unique people: hire them.

Politics. There are those who make things happen, those who watch things happen, and those who say "what happened?" Do not expect geeks to be attuned to corporate politics, or even to know what is going on in the business at large. Make sure their manager is filtering their communications and proposals. A geek will demand a new SAN just as the business reports earnings 50% below estimates, or complain that the team is under-utilised and not appreciated just as layoffs are being planned, or tell the new CIO who moved across from Finance that the users are idiots and never know what they want anyway.

Estimating. Everything looks like "a couple of days" to a geek. They are always 90% done. It is the last bug. How anybody who spends their life immersed in technology (the home range of Murphy's Law) can be so optimistic seems mystifying until one recalls that process and action and time are off their radar. Double everything and get the project managers to look under the hood.

Hoarding knowledge. To geeks, knowledge is personal power, not a group asset. Technical cleverness and indispensability is their antlers, their tusks, their dominance display. Once they return from conferences or training courses, any IP to be disseminated into the rest of the organisation will need to be surgically extracted. Systems of Byzantine complexity will be constructed and nobody else will know how to operate or fix them. Make sure you reward people who share knowledge ("of course she's going to the conference again this year – look at all the good training she ran for us after the last one"). Assign young apprentices to study at the feet of the master. Decline transfers and promotions citing undocumented systems that will fail without them.

Greed and envy. My old boss, Charles Wang of CA, spoke of how most business decision-makers may be driven by the old Fear Uncertainty and Doubt, but technical decision-makers (or recommenders) are also driven by Greed and Envy: FUDGE. Geeks are technophiles. Watch out for the vendor-crafted business case that conceals the only real driver, being that somebody wants one because everyone else has one.

Starting with stuff. There is a wonderful IT implementation model: People Process Technology, in that order. Geeks implement Technology, in that order. Get business analysts, architects and other damage controllers involved in any project, especially one that is a geek's idea. Find the stakeholders (the geek won't have) and see what they think. Don't let the geeks rush off and talk to vendors until the people and process aspects are sufficiently advanced that the organisation can specify what it needs from the technology. The stuff comes last.

Geeks are sensitive delicate creatures, easily ruffled, in many ways helpless. They can also be infuriating, petulant, stubborn and seemingly thick-headed, sometimes destructive. But if you take the time to understand them, know their priorities, and find their motivators, they can be effectively managed to give them personal satisfaction while returning great value. Perhaps we can explore that more another day. For now you can use these twelve watch points in order to keep them behind the fence, to move breakable objects out of the way, and to minimise damage to the business.

Seven Steps for Managing Geeks

In the previous article we categorised people working in IT into two groups: those who are oriented around action (process, business, projects) and those who are oriented around things (hardware and software technology, documents, data). Geeks are the IT staffers who are more interested in technology than the business drivers to use it. For the health of the business it's most important that management understand the geek mentality and manage appropriately. To get you started, we pointed out the most important threats to watch out for from geek culture. Now we move on to really managing geeks: how to get the best from your geeks and to help them grow.

The days of the pure technologist are on the wane. Like other specialist professions before them they are slowly becoming of lower value and less esteem. As the business aspects of IT gain prominence - and as IT matures into a new professionalism - it is the analysts and architects and systems engineers who step into the limelight. Geeks need to grow to retain their value to the business and their personal satisfaction. This growth needs to be sideways into broader skills, not deeper into technology. The ones who do not, or can not, escape the technology silo will be increasingly marginalised, and displaced by young usurpers.

Having geeks retreat into their cubicles or wander off to another employer or get themselves laid off is a terrible waste of corporate IP. Nurture them for their unique technical skills but grow them out and cycle more in else they become stale and venomous and develop an inflated sense of their own worth. With proper management the corporate intellectual property grows while the individuals do too. So here are seven steps to manage and grow your geeks. I designed and ran four-day workshops in a major corporate, combining steps 2, 3 and 4 below, which trained 88 people. Average score on "use of my time" was 4.5 out of 5, "impact on your thinking/behaviour/direction" 4, and "return on investment for the company" 4. All managers reported an average positive change.

1) You need to care. You may care because they are your friends and colleagues. You may care because they represent a large investment that needs to make a corresponding return. You may care because losing them from the business is a loss of corporate knowledge. For whatever reason, the satisfaction and growth of geeks should be of primary concern to all good managers.

2) Rattle their cage. Geeks are often complacent, secure in the knowledge that they alone wrote the Pearl scripts, they alone can restart the nightly batch run. They welcome the pager in the night (though they protest) because it is a loud validation of their own importance and indispensability. We know it isn't true. We know when they go someone else will step into the breach, learn what is needed, and after a period of chaos order will be restored. If they get too expensive and useless we take that hit. So you must shake their security. A round of layoffs helps. In any case, run a compulsory workshop on career planning. Make it very personal: it is for them and about them. Start by laying out the hard facts:

- Professions decline (look at telephonists, typists and steam engine drivers; recently, think DBAs, sysprogs and programmers).

- Everyone gets older and slower, yet at the same time more expensive. At what point can they be displaced by a college kid at half the price?
- A technologist will probably be doing the same thing in ten years – the career options are limited. Most don't want to be managers and would not enjoy it or make a good job of it. Get them to visualise being in the same job.

Help them see themselves as you and the company sees them: as a productive unit. Explain how their salary must be justified by the value they return. If their value does not increase, then their salary will not either. Walk though how that value is measured: not in technical genius but in results, productivity, versatility, and keeping up with change. Challenge them that there is a whole world they are unaware of.

There are three kinds of people: those that make things happen, those that watch things happen, and those who say "what happened?" Geeks tend to be in the latter group. Explain that they may choose not to play the corporate power and politics games, but they owe it to themselves to at least be aware of what is going on. Test them on company directions and strategies. Examine the real financial state of the company. Reveal some power groups and games being played.

IT is about business as much as technology now. Get them to examine the questions: What kind of people does the company want in IT now? In ten years? What skills are most useful? Discuss career options: business analyst, architect, consultant, management, dropping out (you are better off encouraging them to go than having Scott Adam's Wally working for you)...

Finish by helping them create a personal development plan.

3) Teach them to take risks. Geeks tend to be risk averse (despite what your Change Manager says), especially outside their technical space. They don't like operating on imperfect information ("I can't do that, I haven't had the training"). Run some exercises, and no it doesn't have to be abseiling. Impromptu speaking is good. So is throwing unknown technologies at them under pressure. Or drama. Deep end them, get them out of the comfort zone.

4) Teach them to sell themselves. Geeks tend to be quiet achievers. Because they often have a certain level of contempt for management (that's you), and for self-aggrandisement, they don't always publicise their own successes. They don't present well on first meeting. They don't inspire confidence in internal or external customers they work with. Run another workshop: how not to get laid off. When the axe falls, the people who survive are:

- The ones that management see contributing
- The ones that the customers give good feedback on, and ask for
- The ones that the CEO liked when she met them

Practice the "elevator sell": they meet the CEO in the corridor, or they are taken in to see a client's CIO "just to introduce you": what do they say? Role play it one at a time in front of the group: shake hands, the "CEO" says "who are you?" and they are on. 10 seconds, go! If they blow it, sit down to ponder while someone else has a go, but they can try again.

Practice making a pitch. Everyone sells: the project manager seeking more resource, the architect delivering their solution, the manager addressing their team. So train them in sales skills and drill them.

5) Foster the growth plans they have made; coach their career planning. Hopefully the plans have changed after steps 3 and 4. Fund as much training as the company can bear (and buffer them from the demands of the business while they are on training – don't let the urgent ruin the important). Make it diverse, not just technology. Help them take opportunities to try something else: temporary assignments, projects, locums, permanent transfers. A stifled and frustrated geek is of less value to you than a free one mentoring their replacement. Now you have two geeks; the new one doing the job and the one who can step back in an emergency. Which leads to the most important step of all...

6) Have a real mentoring program. You can't have the same geek in the same chair for a decade. They will go feral or get bored and leave. The only way to retain their IP (despite what software vendors tell you) is to have them pass it on to understudies. This requires management support, a managed program, mentor and mentee education, time allocated, effectiveness monitoring, and reward and recognition.

7) Finally, make the best of the ones who just don't get it. Some geeks are beyond remediation. Eventually they will become so embittered or lazy or openly contemptuous that you will have to fire them, but with careful management you can still get a long period of productivity from them first. Keep them technically challenged. Give them toys to play with. But reward delivery of results. Slap down prima-donna behaviour. Try not to let them get the wagons in a circle: don't let a geek clique form. They must respect customers and management, or at least behave like they do. If you are

fortunate enough to employ the happy, well-adjusted geek, content to potter away for ever, committed to customer satisfaction, focused on results, then treasure them.

Inside the geek

Every discussion of human behaviour requires simplification or generalisation. Stereotypes can still be useful models. One such model is the geek. Many IT people fit the model, even if each one brings their own individual twist to it.

Behold the geek

It does not speak

Social skills it lacks

It attacks

It is particularly charmed

By a server farm

And when things abends

It mends

(With apologies to Ogden Nash)

So let us examine the stereotypical geek. How can we separate out the simplified model from the complexity of observed behaviours? To carve an elephant from marble, remove everything that is not-elephant.

Put another way, there are two kinds of people: those who divide the human race into two kinds and those who don't. So we look for some characteristics that distinguish the geek from the not-geek.

Here are some models for categorising people:

- People process technology: no question where geeks fit in this popular model.

- Masculine / feminine: there are a few female geeks, but there is something very male about geek: analytical not instinctual, logical not emotional.

- Target Account Selling®[1] (TAS) looks at what motivates people to make a decision. In an earlier 'classic' version of TAS, people fell into four groups, driven by relationships, business, technical, or money. Geeks fall neatly into the third category.

- Dominance, Influence, Steadiness, Conscientiousness: DiSC®[2] is a more fundamental parser of people, and geeks show up less clearly, but they do tend to cluster around "C": strongly skewed towards introverted, less clearly so towards task-oriented.

- Myers-Briggs Type Indicator®[3] (MBTI): of the 16 possible profiles, geeks fit the following ... oh forget it. MBTI is very useful when you can spend a day on it to build a team. For casual discussion like this it is over the top.

One characteristic of the geek is a low Emotional Intelligence (EQ). Whether it is a blindness or a naivety is debatable, but they cope badly with complex emotional situations: conflict, power struggles, divided loyalties, suffering. They will withdraw, and put up shields of cynicism, callousness or aggression.

Geeks are politically naïve. Not only do they not participate in office politics but they seldom see it, let alone understand it. I recommend TAS or similar training for all geeks, whether they work in sales or

[1] http://www.thetasgroup.com/
[2] http://www.discprofile.com/
[3] http://www.myersbriggs.org/

not, as a system for dissecting political structures. The lights go on for many geeks (including the author) when politics is subject to logical systematic analysis.

Geeks eschew the sordid business of money, especially of selling. But everybody sells (or needs to sell): ideas, projects, themselves. Geeks tend to be awful at sales. Any logical system that teaches them why and how to sell will open their eyes and expand their world view, thereby benefiting the company and their own personal development

Distaste for capitalism doesn't mean geeks are always left wing. They can be somewhere to the right of Margaret Thatcher or Charleton Heston. But extreme positions are typical: it is all symptomatic of that childishly simplistic world view.

Geeks think everything can be resolved with logical analysis. They think if they show a clear logical argument why it ought to be this way, and say so loudly for long enough, people will suddenly see the light.

>Geek: "It ought to be this way…"

>Boss: "Sure it should but it isn't"

>Geek: "But it should be! If only people would…"

Then they get frustrated and decide everybody is stupid when this doesn't work. Eventually this develops into terrible cynicism and in the end they dissociate from the community of the business.

Geeks respect knowledge. To establish pecking order they play that machismo playground boy thing of who can out-fact the other.

>"No, Jupiter comes before Saturn, dummy".

>"I think you'll find the Camaro has the 352 engine".

"Gimme a non-directional 17 inch flange, and make sure it has the knurled outer lip."

"That model Compaq has a 100MHz front side bus, so this isn't going to work"

On first meeting they quickly determine whether one is speaking geek, and whether one expresses an interest in important subjects, i.e. things. If you attempt to speak in geek, some will be honoured by your efforts but most will, like the French, treat your stumbling with contempt. Don't try to bluff it.

Prima donnas are common among geeks. When I managed a team of technical people there were geeks. I was inclined to indulge the prima donna complex in return for a quiet life, but having raised a child I'd be less inclined to tolerate it now. Humour them and they'll just get worse.

Another aspect of the geek is arrested development: they can be quite immature. Prima donna-ism is just spoilt childishness. Grow them up a bit. One way to do that is to fire them: geeks don't get enough of that.

Geeks love problems. They savour them, relish them – they are connoisseurs of problems. Like a tiger hunter they admire them before killing them. Then they re-tell the story for years to come. The best problems are technology ones because they are almost always solvable by rational analysis and the application of the geek's skills and experience. Process problems are good too, because problems are good, and because process can be deconstructed rationally. People problems are less good, because people are messy unpredictable creatures, so geeks tend to shy away from such problems, which is one more reason why they often make poor managers.

One unfortunate aspect of their affection for problems is their delight in sharing them, even at the most inappropriate moments, such as in meetings with clients or executives.

What are their strengths?

- Intelligence: geeks often have a high IQ (but see EQ, above)

- Problem solving and general analytical ability: if you want something fixed or dissected, put a geek on it.

- Diligence (if they haven't been spoilt): geeks hate being beaten by inanimate objects or processes – they will gnaw on a task until it is resolved.

- A delight in delivering an outcome: the tougher the better. Geeks are technology finishers.

- Honesty and openness: lack of guile. What you see is what you get, which is not always an attractive prospect.

It will be evident that the author has quite a patronising attitude to geeks. They do themselves and the organisation harm with their conviction of their own brilliance and their stubborn inability to see how narrow a field they excel in. One of my job tasks has been to find career paths for geeks. The truth is there are none beyond Senior Geek until they can grow up.

As we have discussed in previous articles, steps must be taken to protect the organisation from the geeks, and then to protect them from themselves by helping them to grow beyond geekishness. Or to minimise the damage if they cannot and will not grow.

Geeks are real. Understand them and they become useful contributors to the business, and you can manage their personal growth.

Species of geek

There are many species of geek. We categorise the family *geekae*:

The guru

This guy can read hex. Over the phone.

Designs an application in his head and codes it over the weekend.

The pundit

Ask him anything and he knows the answer. Ask him to do anything and wait.

The wizard

The Wizard fixes where everyone else failed. He can get Linux to talk to a coffee pot. He can fix software from alien spaceships. He can install Acrobat and stop Windows updates.

The terrier

The terrier geek never gives up. Weeks after everyone else went off and implemented the alternative, they emerge unshaven and pale with a result.

The tinker

Always twiddling, trying to get things to work. Often because he broke them.

The slave

Works 25x8. There when you leave, still there when you come back in the morning.

The wonk

Organised the Service Desk. Built the Change process. Rostered the kitchen cleaning. Runs the social club. Rings his wife every day at 11;10.

The space cadet

Is writing a new script for Elvish tongue. Eats cold bean salad from the can. Sharpens pencils under a crystal pyramid.

The hermit

Stays in his cube behind piles of papers and books. Runs away when spoken to. Misses most meetings including those involving cake.

The worry

Collects Nazi memorabilia. Fires semi-automatic weapons for a hobby. Has been warned several times about knives at work. Bugs his girlfriend's flat. Often looks like he (always he) hasn't slept in a week. Sometimes just stares instead of talking.

The bluffer

Can't read hex. Can't read PHP. Can't read English. Knows a thousand words of jargon, and uses them often and incorrectly. Makes up acronyms then blusters when called on them.

The duffer

Older than IBM. Worked on the Apollo space program. Wears a tie and cardigan. Very nice and entirely useless.

The improbable

One of the best software developers I ever knew is an ex-welder who looks like a Lord of the Rings dwarf extra. He sounds illiterate – and could be for all I know – but he cuts code with the best.

Another developer from the mainframe days drank bourbon in his office and often slept with his feet on the desk. He spoke in grunts. One client company still worships the baseball cap he left behind.

The Bill Gates

Bill created his own genre of geek. Happy retirement Bill.

The Geeks Will Have to Get it

Business thinking is filtering through IT. Soon IT will be part of the business and everyone in IT will have to think that way. The geeks might struggle with this.

The concept of business-IT alignment is well accepted. It even has its own acronym, bITa. It is so well accepted that we are on to the next big thing: business-IT *integration*. "Alignment" is, like, so 2007.

Whatever you call it, the concept that IT needs to work for the business, with the business and ultimately *in* the business is well entrenched.

The IT Service Management (ITSM) movement is driven by the demand for bITa. ITSM is IT's response to business expectation that IT will think in business terms, communicate in business terms, and most of all spend money in business terms instead of technological ones.

There has been a change in the nature of CIOs over the past decade, from the days when most CIOs came up through the technical ranks and many of them never understood the business, to today when most CIOs are outward-facing business people who represent IT in the executive councils of the organisation. The day-to-day running of IT is delegated to operational managers – fewer CIOs are hands on. And more often than not they have come in from outside IT to run it.

Certainly we still have a ways to go. CIOInsight.com[1] reports that "Just 31 percent of the 281 CIOs we polled have earned an MBA... (Most CIOs instead earned degrees in science, math and engineering.)" But I think a third of CIOs with an MBA would be a lot higher than in 1998, and certainly would exceed that of 1988!

---

[1] http://blogs.cioinsight.com/research_central/content001/cios/do_cios_need_an_mba_1.html

The trends are positive. IT strategic plans tend to be informed by the business strategic plan instead of Windows releases or the advent of new technologies. A concept growing in popularity is that there is no such thing as an IT strategic plan, just the IT part of the business plan.

So CIOs get it. They understand that IT has to think as part of the business. They grok business.

Among the next tier down of IT management, my experience is that the level of "business-grok" is variable. IT managers range from suits to geeks. Some know the business, some know that they don't know the business, and some don't even know what it is they ought to know.

A Hybrid Manager is "A person with strong technical skills and adequate business knowledge or vice versa" (Dr. Michael Earl). According to Dr. David Skyrme[1], the term Hybrid Manager was first coined in the 1980s! We have been waiting a long time.

So CIOs are grokking business. IT managers are a mixed bag. What about the workers? There seems to be no research of this question, but common perception is that the shift has only just begun. A few people talk the talk, but the culture of almost all IT organisations is not a business-centric one. The geeks don't grok business.

ITSM is playing a role in getting the message across. Many people think ITSM is about improving service or saving money. It isn't. It usually improves service and it just might save some money, but the purpose of Service Management (of anything) is to get deliverers thinking in terms of customers. In IT we hope this will better align IT with the business.

IT is a pipe, pumping information services out to users. If we can plan and act and measure in terms of what comes out of the pipe instead of what we need in order to get it there, then we are

---

[1] http://www.skyrme.com/insights/6hybrid.htm

thinking in the customer's terms instead of our own internal frame of reference.

Along this road there are three levels of maturity in IT thinking:

Inward oriented

"We need to improve the network infrastructure because these switches are overloaded, and that subnet keeps failing. Give me $200,000."

"We have to give priority to a project that contributes to our standard architecture"

Customer oriented

"Application response times are lower than the agreed service level, and the major constraint right now is network capacity. In addition, availability is way down for users on the third floor because of repeated network outages. Give me $200,000."

"It's a good idea but what service will it improve?"

Business oriented

"Sales department have orders backup up so far they have hired a temp. They reckon we are losing customers because of it. One major cause is the slow response times. And it is not helping that their phone sellers are on the third floor, where we keep losing connectivity. Give me $200,000 and we can get rid of the temps, pump sales and keep customers happy."

"That is the Brokerage system that is struggling – our most profitable. Let's get on it."

The widespread sheep-dipping of staff through ITIL Foundations training is one step along the road. Some people come out of that training like religious converts. But it is still generally agreed that the "People" part of ITIL's "four Ps" of People Process Products and Partners is much neglected. We design the processes and we buy the tools but we often fail to execute the cultural change so that they are embraced and used and kept alive and grown.

We cannot measure the three levels of maturity in terms of processes in books or tools installed. It is the maturity of the culture that matters. What words do people use? How do they prioritise their actions? Who do they communicate with and how? There is a lot of attention at the moment on this idea of People in ITSM – look at conference agendas. It is not because we are doing such a good job that causes this attention.

Even if we were getting people to think in Service terms, that is only the second level of maturity: customer centric. The model is still us-and-them – it is just that we now care about "them" and the service we give them.

Getting to that second level is not such a big ask for most IT people. It is still a formal relationship: based on SLAs, measured analytically, treating the customer as a black box.

Thinking at third level maturity is much harder. This is a "we" mentality. IT *is* the business - however you like to frame it: IT does business improvement; IT engineers business information; IT is the business engine. As a recent article[1] said ""The average hard nosed CFO is not going to be impressed with achieving objectives at huge, out of budget costs, or indeed have delivery of great internal customer service with no regard to the financial implications."

---

[1] http://www.prlog.org/10039995-parity-reveals-significant-lack-of-business-skills-among-it-managers.pdf

Especially for the geeks within IT, the whole business universe can seem alien and not a little repulsive. But soon the organisation will no longer tolerate IT people who do not wish to understand or participate, any more than they would tolerate sales people who feel that way.

Right now, it falls to middle managers and architects and business analysts and client relationship managers and a raft of others to "translate from business to technology" and vice versa. The very fact that we need this function indicates two things: that we are not at third level maturity and that we are pandering to the geeks. It is not the organisation's job to translate to people who cannot or will not understand. It is every employee's responsibility to understand what their business is saying to them. It is true there is an onus on non-IT people, especially managers, to understand as much about IT as they can where it is relevant to them, but the purpose is to make informed decisions, not to bridge a culture and communication gap.

The future is that IT staff will have to understand the organisation they are employed by: what its goals are, what its strategy is, what are the current tactics to get there, what are the immediate priorities, who matters around here, and how things ought to be done. And they will have to consider themselves part of it.

I heard a lovely story at a conference recently but I am sorry I cannot recall who to credit it with. A group of business people was touring an American private hospital. They met a man in a white coat in the corridor. They asked him what he did.

"I help people get well."

"Are you a doctor?" "No." "A nurse?" "No." "Well what then?"

"I am a janitor. I clean the toilets. I make sure they are free from organisms that would delay the recovery of our patients."

That is being part of the business.

You have the pager for Christmas

As IT becomes just another profession and pay rates trend down from the astronomical, IT employees will expect to have more of a life outside work, and to be rewarded when work intrudes.

In the last millennium, Information Technology was the cutting edge career for the nation's best and brightest. It was acceptable to work long hours and weekends. It was acceptable to have dinners, movies and children's sports interrupted by the pager or mobile phone. It was acceptable to work late at home processing emails. This was the price we paid for **money and prestige.**

As IT matures, it is discovering professionalism, certification, process and discipline. As a result it is becoming as exciting as chemical engineering and not as well paid. Now the majority of IT workers are considered advanced clerical functions. Being "in IT" does not hold the same cachet it once did. Now we say it in a bored voice, like, you know, in IT.

In order to make the future trend clear, consider this: some of the most prestigious highly trained technical careers in past centuries included typist, telephonist, steam engine driver, welder, and DBA.

IT pay rates are high, but not all of them, and many have been fairly static for some time. While "leading edge" skills demand good dollars, some IT skills and roles are becoming run of the mill, and paid accordingly. Take a look at network or PC or web/internet related roles in this IT Career Planet article[1].

So it is no longer reasonable to expect 24-hour slavery from IT employees. They don't get paid enough and they don't get enough prestige and glory as a result.

---

[1] http://www.itcareerplanet.com/salarytrends/article.php/3733826

Management have not noticed yet for some strange reason. What some IT workers do is nothing short of heroic.

This is particularly true of support people, but developers have been known to pull all-weekend stints to finish a system, and even managers occasionally go on a training course on a Saturday (although it is OK for them to leave early after encouraging the troops). Service Desk people tend to be on a roster but it is not unknown for life to be disrupted when it is all hands to the pump for an extended Severity 1 outage or a major system release.

Applications support staff carry a varying burden depending on their organisation. Some applications run as smoothly as the proverbial baby's bottom. Others are more like what comes out of it. Some apps staff have it easy; many more wince when the mobile phone rings or pager buzzes.

The pinnacle of IT heroism, though, is the IT Operations staff. They regularly work long and odd hours, either to make changes outside normal work times, or to turn out as Level 1 and 2 support engineers to resolve incidents. Once again the depth varies depending on the employer organisation, but in general Operations staff accept disruption of their personal lives that most people would find intolerable.

Not only are they doing this for less money and lower prestige, but attitudes are changing too. It is no longer fashionable to work yourself to death. Even the Japanese are talking about work-life balance. Nowadays, some Operations people even have other interests besides work. No, really.

While the idea of techies breeding is a cause for concern in some circles, a proportion of them have families.

As some IT roles become common, or considered common, they are falling prey to that nemesis of IT, unions. Unions have funny ideas about occupational health, and maternity/paternity leave, and sleep.

So even for the intractable IT stalwarts who only leave their desk for calls of nature and insufficient sleep the writing is on the wall. Their spouses, friends, shop stewards, peers and even some employers want them to get a life.

This will have interesting implications for the job market when staff say "Sorry but I have other plans on Saturday" or "I have a thousand days in lieu owing and I want to start taking them" or "We want an hourly rate for overtime".

Firemen and cops are heroes, but only during their shift (major disasters excepted). Doctors only put up with this crap for a few years as interns. Power plant operators don't do it.

Certainly, someone has to carry the pager for Christmas. But in future they will be more likely to be on shift, working, than an after-hours "volunteer".

Granted, few IT staff do complain. Well actually most of them complain, but only in the same way that people complain about the weather, or ads on TV. Few push back, or walk away. But every year some do walk away, or burn out, and with them goes priceless experience, not to mention their knowledge of undocumented systems.

Perhaps younger people who haven't been steeped in that culture will see it differently in the coming decade. Employers will need to see it differently. And we all might get some sleep.

An innovative approach to corporate training

IT organisations have always had a refreshingly innovative approach to business practices, willing to try new techniques unconstrained by traditional modes of thinking.

In this spirit, some are experimenting with new approaches to maximise the return on investment from corporate offsite training events. These events are extremely expensive by most business training standards. They involve flights, hotels, and removing revenue generating employees from the field for days on end.

As a result, it is imperative that the return to the business from these events be maximised.

Frustrated by the dated thinking in this area, some organisations have taken a new tack, aggressively embracing sleep deprivation as a modality for ensuring optimal results from training.

This paper examines early anecdotal evidence of the success of this technique, and recommends further more rigorous experimentation to validate these results.

Methodology

The subject (the author) was awakened at 5:00 on day 1, awakened at 4:00 on day 2, kept at maximum mental activity levels until midnight, then awakened again at 7:00 on Day 3. Training was delivered on Days 2 and 3. In order to maximise the benefit of sleep deprivation, additional factors were introduced:

- The subject was flown to one city early on Day 1 and to a second early on Day 2, through three time-zones.
- The subject was required to share a room on the night of Day 2 with another employee.

The methodology of the experiment has been criticised on two counts.

First the subject was allowed some degree of sleep both nights. In the company's defence it must be pointed out that the only alternative flights between the two cities (on the afternoon of Day 1) would have allowed the subject to sleep in the same city for two contiguous nights and to get at least five hours more sleep on the night of Day 2, thus seriously diminishing the effect of the experiment.

Second, other unconventional training techniques such as the Information Barrage, Zero Application of Learning, and Sustained Bullet Point Recitation were used at the same time, making it difficult to isolate the value of each technique.

Results

Careful testing of the subject's retention of materials delivered during the two days of training have identified clear recall of at least 17 distinct words, and the names of three presenters and one product.

Comparison with the control group of those subjects resident locally - and allowed to sleep at home - actually shows higher retention levels among the controls. But the experimenters contend the results are influenced by Post-Prandial Carousing which was applied more extensively to the experimental subjects than to the controls.

Once the results have been corrected to account for this factor, the difference falls below levels of statistical significance, and may even show a net positive for the sleep-deprived subjects.

It is this result that we recommend deserves much more rigorous experimental attention to confirm the real benefits of sleep deprivation for learning reinforcement.

Conclusion

It is clear to the author that the IT industry is breaking new ground in Adult Learning, with a creative new approach that seems to be delivering results of interest from the rigorous application of Sleep Deprivation.

Despite the fact that this technique contradicts almost all currently accepted thinking among Adult Learning experts, the industry has never allowed itself to be constrained by orthodoxy.

Obviously such a large and successful industry would not make such massive investments in training and then apply such a radical technique if it didn't see the benefits clearly. It behoves the academic world to look more closely at the phenomenon happening here, to carry these new discoveries to the wider community.

About the author:

The IT Skeptic is the pseudonym of Rob England, an IT consultant and commentator. Although he works around the ITIL industry, he is self-employed and his future is not dependant on ITIL – he has nothing to sell you but the ideas in this book.

He has twenty years experience mapping business requirements to IT solutions, ten of them in service management. (Some readers will be relieved to learn that this book reveals what "service management" means). He is active in the itSMF (the professional body for ITIL). He is the author of a popular blog www.itskeptic.org and a number of internet articles taking a critical look at IT's absurdities, especially those relating to ITIL. He is also a paid-up Skeptic. He lives with his wife and son in a small house in a small village.

Also by the IT Skeptic:

Introduction to Real ITSM

It is not often that ITSM books are funny, but - according to readers - this one is funny.

This book is not about ITIL®. Really. Real ITSM is a tongue-in-cheek satirical look at what the real-life processes of IT Service Management might be, as compared to the "official" defined processes published in the authorised books of frameworks like ITIL. Find out what the Service Desk are really up to. The Introduction to Real ITSM is not all lampooning the status quo in IT. It also promotes a number of alternate ideas to stimulate discussion.

See more Realitsm at www.realitsm.com

Owning ITIL

This book is essential reading for **all decision makers** (IT-literate or not) who are presented with an ITIL® proposal or asked to oversee an ITIL project, or find something called "ITIL" or "Service Management" in their budget. It tells you what the ITIL industry won't. For **everyone else involved in ITIL** projects, this book will help you stay grounded and safe.

The book explains, in lay-manager's terms, **what ITIL is**. It reveals what ITIL is **good** for, what it is **bad** at, what to **expect** from it. It describes how to ensure an ITIL project **succeeds**, what to look for in the **business case**, and how to measure the **results**.

See www.itskeptic.org/owningitil

The Worst of the IT Skeptic

A compilation of writings from the first three years of the IT Skeptic so that you can conveniently read the wickedest wackiest wittiest posts of your favourite IT bombast.

The IT Skeptic's blog at www.itskeptic.org is a commentary on IT's sillier moments, especially those related to ITSM in general and ITIL in particular. This is not because the IT Skeptic wishes to focus on ITIL - it is just that ITIL and itSMF provide such great material for a skeptic.

This material is delivered to you in a special media presentation technology known as a "book": affordable, flexible, robust, light, compact, wireless, with a remarkably low power consumption, zero boot time, integral bookmarking and annotation functions, permitted on airplanes even during takeoff and landing, and readable in daylight.

See www.itskeptic.org/worst

The IT Skeptic Looks At CMDB

Available as a digital download or in print, this book lays out the IT Skeptic's arguments against CMDB as defined in ITIL. Get yourself a concise, structured discussion of why CMDB is a bad idea for most businesses. Wave this book around at the next meeting!

See http://www.itskeptic.org/node/1375

He Tangata

To be published in 2009

See www.itskeptic.org/hetangata

www.ingramcontent.com/pod-product-compliance
Lightning Source LLC
Chambersburg PA
CBHW071226050326
40689CB00011B/2477